Already Here:
the matter of Love

Already Here:
the matter of Love

Kelly Corbet

ISBN: 1522731083
ISBN 13: 9781522731085
Library of Congress Control Number: 2015920724
CreateSpace Independent Publishing Platform
North Charleston, South Carolina
Cover photograph by Stano Scepan. I chose sunflowers because of their natural inclina-
tion to follow the light. They offer a fabulous heliotropic metaphor!

To my much-loved children and godchildren,
Nolan, Will, Mateus, Quinn, Alison, Lola, Malia, Ava, and Ella Mae:

Thank you for your patience and Love.

Clap along if you feel like happiness is the truth.

—Pharrell Williams,
"Happy"

Acknowledgments

⁓

I BELIEVE WE CHOOSE OUR parents. Before we slap on a body, complete with ego and forgetfulness, we select the important people who can help deliver us to the lessons we need. I must have had "compassion examples required" on my "Learn This" list because my so-thankful-for-them parents showed me compassion through uncountable deeds and silent kindnesses. Their way of being in the world—treating everyone as special and valuable— permeated my own way of being in the world, and I am very, very grateful to have witnessed that. I would not have been able to write this book without such a beautiful foundation.

My husband deserves an ultra-super-mega medal for managing to live with me successfully all these years. Shamelessly uxorious, he is my staunchest supporter, my biggest lesson-learning partner, and my best friend.

I feel so very blessed by all the thinkers and writers and beautiful souls who made it their business to share their brilliance with the rest of us. Where would we be without them? I'm glad we don't know.

Contents

Think Again

THIS IS A LITTLE BOOK about the big power of Love to restore us to our joyous, true selves. It delivers proof and more proof that we create what we see and experience. To really appreciate these pages, it's probably best to jettison many elderly preconceptions and open up brain space for radically different thoughts. What you're about to catch a glimpse of will probably not match your habitual life MO.

Oh, and I should warn you: the contents—the *language* of this book—may look, well, "fluffy." That is only because of a defect in our preestablished concepts of strength, power, and success. Contrary to popular thinking, remembering our innate joy makes us *stronger, more* robust, and *more* wildly successful than anything else ever could. No boot camp, ivy-flanked graduate school or hike to a far-flung summit is required.

Similar to a DIY,[1] but more a BTY—back to yourself—book, it offers concrete examples of how to Love ourselves and each other back to our natural way of being ("miserable" is *not* our natural state…as babies constantly attempt to remind us!). In fact, the title, *Already Here*, is a spoiler alert to our truth: the Love we are is already here, kindly and patiently waiting for us to recognize it.

---

1 Do it yourself.

There isn't, thankfully, one single way to Love. Included here are *some* ways: my ways. And even if they don't all ring your bell, knowing about the possibility of them—and the Love they invite—will certainly open your own possibilities to new leagues.

I share personal stories and techniques that have powerfully worked for me and many indulgent friends, family members, and people I don't even know, in very short pockets of time. Sometimes three minutes are all we need to reframe our perspective to include more Love. I am certain that many (maybe all) the exercises can work for you, too. **Love's power is undeniable!** The exercises will help you experience *in your own body* just what I mean. This is important because, if you are like most people, you may doubt pure Love's abilities to hook you up with a totally happy life. We're kinda out of practice, so feeling it in our bodies—sensing it physically—makes it seem more "real" for now. (After you've practiced awhile, you will be surprised at how "unimportant" our bodies actually are, but more on that later!) Even if you have not carried around buckets of overflowing joy in your life, it is not too late, nor is it impossible to start intimately knowing happiness this very day. All we need to do is think again...and learning to "rethink" is really the purpose of this book.

Now, I live in a state where liquor isn't sold on Sunday until *after* church lets out, so you can imagine my surprise to discover that *rethinking* was the earliest definition for "repent." In its original classical Greek,[2] repent—μετανοέω, or *metanoeó*—isn't about moral shortcomings or hell-if-you-don't. It does *not* mean "Stop that and feel bad about yourself, you worthless sinner!" *Metanoeó* comes from "change after being with" (*meta*), and "to think" (*noeó*). Truly, in repenting, we undergo a "profound transformation," a "conversion." In essence, "repent" in its initial form (prior to

---

2 There is still debate about the word, so depending on which scholar you believe, which original language is applied, or which dictionary is most dependable, you may adhere to a completely different meaning. For the sake of expediency, let's just follow this etymological path for now.

Latin's political and moral repurposing) is to think about something later and change one's mind—*think* differently and therefore *be* different.

Doesn't that piece of insight spin the dial 180 degrees?

Not that I have been big into repenting as it is currently interpreted these days, but I find so much wisdom and inspiration in the origins of that word (and more than a little irony, given its current use). Experience has proven to me that changing my own mind—intentionally transforming how I perceive things—is the most powerful and direct way I've encountered joy. For me, *joy is the essence of true spirituality* and is a much greater metric for "holiness" than, say, confessing one's sins, followed by absolution with a hair shirt,[3] or at the very least, feeling like a big piece of poop for not correctly adhering to dogma. Spirituality is not about turning away from the bad stuff and "repenting," according to its popular meaning. Spirituality is consciously turning *toward* the good stuff and embracing the bliss that's practically sitting on our laps, just awaiting our attention.

Finding our joy requires no leaping. It only wishes we'd opt for being lifted.

So many smart and thoughtful people—friends, religious figures, philosophers, and mystics—assert that finding bliss demands "necessary suffering," years of "arduous meditation," or that it is "exquisitely difficult."

---

3 A hair shirt is an undergarment—said to predate written history—made of goat hair, or something prickly and uncomfortable to wear as a sinner's penance. All sorts have donned them, supposedly, from Ivan the Terrible to Mother Teresa. My hair shirts are always mental.

But I say that true grace, joy, bliss, or oneness[4] derives from just changing our minds. Admittedly, this may call for a bit of brain training—oh, how we love our habits—but once you get the gist, you will probably laugh at how easy it is (or how hard we have made it)!

Does it sound nutty? If peace within were really so simple to achieve, why are *so* many of us *so* miserable? Or even just nonjoyous? Good question, but that's for another bottle of wine (hint: it probably has to do with forgetting). More important than that is remembering how to leave misery in the dust by simply releasing into the patient joy vibration of who we really are. And there's nothing crazy about that.

Thankfully, getting to grace—or at least its front porch—doesn't need to take long, and there are no prerequisites (except for being in a body, which, I presume, you are...and if you aren't, then you probably already know about the grace thing). You need not wait until the kids go to college, or you've lost those last five pounds to make room for huge joy—and what many call miracles. You can learn to change your mind (or *rediscover*) how to connect at a consciousness-penetrating level in less time than it takes to watch a rerun of your favorite sitcom.

Maybe even less time than that! When I began serious research for this book, conscripting innocents to practice the (mostly) three-minute exercises and report back, one very wise woman responded, "Three minutes? Who doesn't have three minutes? I *always* have three minutes." She's right. In about as much time as it takes to eat a breakfast taco or organize your wallet, you could be opening the door to bliss, happiness, or any number of better-than-whatcha-got-going-on-now options.

---

4 I use these words interchangeably, hoping to keep us from getting caught up by a single word, and look instead toward the direction these words point. I find words stunningly insufficient in expressing the truth, or even its pieces. Sort of ironic for a writer, I know, but until we can move beyond words, I'll summon the most helpful ones I know!

Gratefully, I am not alone in the ideas I share here, and I shamelessly invoke the wisdom of more intelligent others who have "rethought" the script they see enacted all around them. (In fact, not a single concept in this book is "new news.") I have called on them frequently to lavish their own truthy words on us. You will recognize many—Jesus, the Buddha, Einstein, and the Beatles. Besides the famous names included, many a brilliant Love sage you will read here may be new to your library of experience, demonstrating that we don't have to be a big name to be a big "repenter" or rethinker of life!

If you already find joy in 99.3 percent of your waking moments, thank you! You found the key. You *remember.* Please, continue being inspirational to us all. If not, please revel in this book, finding joy where you least expected it: here and now! If you've read so far, you may find some valuable ideas within these pages. That is my sincere desire.

To change one's life:

1. **Start immediately.**
2. **Do it** *flamboyantly.*
3. **No exceptions.**

—William James

CHAPTER 1

The Big Four

Nothing is yet in its true form.

—C. S. Lewis

BEFORE DIVING INTO THE DEEP end, I would like to introduce some concepts you may not have spent much time pondering lately. You may not believe them right now—or ever—but for joy's sake, please give them a try! If you open your mind-set to their possibilities, if you repent—*rethink what you believe and change your mind*—you may uncover great and life-altering payoffs.

In consideration of people like my darling and smart friend Abbe, who would rather all help-yourself books be reduced to a single list with bullet points, here are the biggies—the foundational essence of this book:

1. Big Love is the strongest force, and it connects us all.
2. Miracles and bliss are the norm.
3. What you think, you see. Your expectations create your reality.
4. Time is not real, so why spend lots of something that isn't real going somewhere we already are?

Let's look at each one of these concepts in detail.

I. Big Love is the strongest force, and it connects us all.

You can call it God, Love, the Akashic Field, Source, consciousness, ether,[5] or a cheese-and-pickle sandwich...it doesn't matter the teensiest speck of a bit because words are just meager symbols (actually, words are *symbols* of symbols, if you want to get technical, but let's not *just* yet). We are all connected via that vibrational force at a basic and not-generally-seeable-with-our-eyes-but-feelable-with-our-hearts level. Even more than connected to it, **we are Big Love!**

Some may doubt Love's connective power because we currently lack a widespread technological means to measure it, but we don't require a machine to reveal gravity's existence or to confirm that the sun's rays can grow crops. Some forces are most easily acknowledged by their effects. Love is often like that. Listen and become present, and by trusting your intuition, you will access and know Love—no measuring device is necessary! (Besides, measuring is overrated and probably keeps us from checking in with our natural "knowingness" on a regular basis.)

2. Miracles and bliss are the norm.

It doesn't always seem like it, but bliss—bursting with quotidian miracles—*is* our natural state. We just forgot this important fact (momentarily). Almost ironically, their ready availability punts miracles right out of the "miracle" category, but until we all recall that, let's just continue

---

5 You might be wondering, "Did Kelly really reference an 'ether' of sorts?" I did, for lack of a better term (and believe me, we're lacking "better terms" for much of what I'm trying to explain here!). Well then, you may further inquire, "What about the famous 1887 Michelson-Morley experiment, which *proved* there's no such thing as an etheric force?" In response, I first ask you to think about what you know of Love already. You've *felt* it, surely, at some point, even if you weren't touching anyone or anything, true? Besides, failing to find what you look for doesn't mean it isn't real. Perhaps it just means you don't have the right equipment, or you're looking in the wrong place. Not finding Tasmanian devils in my backyard does not prove they do not exist.

naming them miracles. By the end of this book, you will know that you can create what you now call miracles, just by accessing the vibration of Love. And because we are all vibrations of Love at our core, such activities are really as normal as normal can be.

Again, I do not stand unescorted in my treatise of bliss being easy. As far as I can tell, Jesus never proclaimed anything like, "OK, everyone, I know this is going to be tedious, and painful and not the slightest bit of fun, but after years of (necessary) suffering, you may be able to stumble your way into the kingdom of heaven.[6] Maybe. Oh, and don't forget to flog yourself along the way!" Never, not once, did I find that sentiment.[7] He said just the opposite! In this very familiar but not, apparently, very believed passage from Matthew 7:7–8, in fact, he flat-out informs us of the following:

Ask, and it shall be given you; seek, and you will find; knock, and it shall be opened unto you. For every one that asks receives; and he that seeks, finds; and to him that knocks it shall be opened.

That doesn't suggest hardship to me. It sounds simple and oh-so-inclusive! It probably does require that we not play Ding Dong Ditch 'Em once we knock, however. We ought to give some attention to that door being opened. That's when we get to experience miracles and bliss.

---

6 By the way, he was being metaphoric when he spoke of the "kingdom of heaven." It is the "place" we go when we are truly connected to our highest self—or nonself. We arrive "there" through total stillness and surrender. Some extraordinary rethinkers found the "kingdom of heaven" amid genocide, terror, and unimaginable violence. Fortunately, most of us can find it on our sofas, a park bench, or waiting for the kids' tae kwon do class to dismiss.

7 In the canonical Gospel of Mark 8:34, Jesus is quoted as saying, "Whoever wants to be my disciple must deny themselves and take up their cross and follow me." However, "denying yourself" in this sense is similar to what Buddhism cites as the cause for suffering, which is mostly about craving, or lusting after bodily things that are impermanent. Jesus just suggested that we deny our "selfiness" that clings to fear, judgment, anger, or other negative emotions.

3. What you think, you see. Your expectations create your reality.

Photo of Perito Moreno by Bob Weinschenk

I feel a bit deceitful, invoking our meager "knowledge" of physics to support something as infinitely profound as spiritual connectedness. It's kind of like asking a glass of water to stand in for the grandeur of a glacier. If we'd never even *heard* of a glacier—the size, sounds, colors, the feelings it invokes—its sheer *wow-wow-wow!* magnificence cannot be approximated by a small amount of H_2O in a cup. They are, atomistically, the same stuff, but one hints only slightly at the other. So it goes with physics and spirituality. That said, I am not at all above inviting some brilliant minds in quantum theory to provide backup. In fact, I'll call on the famous Werner Heisenberg and his Observer Effect right now to bolster my case that our attention (consciousness) influences matter.

What Heisenberg's Observer Effect tells us is that we cannot observe a system without also af-

fecting the outcome. The most are-you-kidding-why-doesn't-everyone-know-about-this? demonstration of said effect is the Double Slit Experiment (physicists like to call it "the most beautiful" experiment). It basically goes like this: one at a time, electrons (or photons) get shot through a solid plate with two slits. Just beyond the plate is a "detector screen" to record what goes through the slits. Originally, experts all naturally assumed that the electrons, having mass, would hurtle individually and marble-like through one slit or the other, forming a line on the screen behind. Instead, mind-blowingly, the single electron salvo acts like waves, forming interference patterns (rows of light and dark, like ripples in water) with each other! But how is that possible, since only *one* electron was shot at a time? When one of the slits gets removed from the experiment, those tricky electrons form a line on the detector screen, like bullets from a gun would do. So, are electrons matter, or are they waves? Oh, both. Physicists tell us that they are wave-like and particle-like, depending...[8] To add to the confusion, do the electrons "know" when there are two slits instead of one and change their behavior accordingly?

But here's what I consider the exceptionally big hoo-ha of the experiment: when a mechanism is added to observe the quantum conundrum (think of someone waiting with her camera to take a picture each time something hits the screen), the electrons go back to acting like particles, line-like in their expression. The mere act of observation collapses the possibilities of the wave function! Don't worry if the details of this experiment aren't crystal clear in your brain. The bottom line is simply that consciousness affects what we can see.[9]

---

8 Well, not *every* physicist. One of my favorite astrophysicists, the brilliant and very entertaining Richard Conn Henry, says it's a "mental universe." No waves, no particles...I actually agree with him, but such an ultimate perspective requires, for most of us, baby steps (as in the exercises in this book).

9 However, if you *do* want to know more, the clearest explanation I've ever read of this fabulous mystery can be found in *Quantum Physics for Poets*, an outrageously great book by Nobel laureate Leon M. Lederman and Christopher Hill.

I bring up this "most beautiful experiment" mainly to propose that our attention influences the outcome of our most personal experiment: our lives (we are, in a sense, densified gobs of electrons). Adding our emotions to the mix is like sending our intentions FedEx overnight for early morning delivery. As William James, the forward-thinking American psychologist and philosopher put it; we help "create" the truths that we "register." When we notice something in our life (consciously or unconsciously), we collapse the wave-like possibilities into one apparent outcome.

The act of observation collapses the possibilities of the wave function.

Or maybe John Lennon put it best of all: "Reality leaves a lot to the imagination."

4. Time is not real (ask a physicist[10]), so why spend lots of something that isn't real going somewhere we already are?

Despite my contention that physics insufficiencies cannot lead us to the truth, you will see that I kinda like to engage relatively modern physics hypotheses and newly discovered "scientific facts" similarly to how I use my yellow highlighter. Ideas sure get a lot more attention when those sentences are highlighted! And, really, who can deny that quoting Einstein lends plausible brawn to an absurd idea? Besides, this brand of science points the right direction in a common—if not commonly agreed-on—vernacular.

---

10 OK, don't ask Lee Smolin; he wrote a whole book about how time *is* real—I just disagree with his main premise. But most other physicists are on the same time-as-we-think-of-it-is-not-real page…

So, regarding time as a sequential phenomenon, Albert Einstein himself said, "The distinction between the past, present, and future is only a stubbornly persistent illusion." While details differ, numerous other physics bigwigs like Bohr, Feynman, and Hawking have confirmed that what we normal, nonphysicist folks perceive as "time" is something else completely.

If at first an idea isn't absurd,
then there's no hope for it.

—Albert Einstein

I bring up the time-as-illusion concept in the "big four" points of this book for a couple reasons.

First, *the biggest chunk of our thinking and/or beliefs is based on what we know from "the past," and that imposes a huge limitation on our possible happiness!* All our previous experiences and learning—unless we add consciousness to the equation, something most of us hardly ever remember to do—frame our mental options of the "future." As if what we know is all there is. Ha! As I will bring up again (and again, and again, because nobody has yet accused me of being subtle), what we "see" can be way off base and is usually obscured by our assumptions (which can be projected only from our own limited history).

The second reason illusory time gets included in the top four points of this little book is because, somehow, we've conjured up the belief that bliss demands incense-filled decades in a mountainside monastery (or at the very least, plenty of weekend retreats). And generally, the Zen-ish scenarios we imagine tend to preclude time for kid-schlepping, spreadsheets, grocery shopping, or any number of worldly-nesses toward which we devote our efforts (and "time"). But time isn't the main ingredient for bliss. *The main ingredient for bliss is releasing yesterdays and tomorrows, and remembering who we are now.*

Our true joy is like those sunglasses we've been looking for *all over*, suddenly realizing they've been propped on our head during our entire search. They're already there, quietly waiting for us to reach up and realize they were never lost at all. Not being lost, "time" is not what's required to rediscover bliss—only remembering where to look. And really, we all need look no further than the Love that resides within each of us, right where we are. This very instant.

⌒

So, there they are, the four broad points of this entire book. But this *is* a book, after all, not a list to put up on the fridge and then promptly ignore. Plus, I've added what I hope are valuable pointers in the chapters that follow. So, unless this list morphed its way into your essence (which is certainly possible; see point #2), I hope you will luxuriate in the chapters and exercises, finding joy in the happy realization that you are closer than you think.

Grace isn't waiting to be cashed in like a "good-deeds bond," and heaven is not a promissory pursuit!

CHAPTER 2

Love: All You Need

Someday, after mastering the winds, the waves,
the tides and gravity,
we shall harness for God the energies of love,
and then, for a second time in the history of the world,
man will have discovered fire.

—*Pierre Teilhard de Chardin*

All you need is love.

—*John Lennon*

John Lennon was right about so many things, not the least of which is that all we need really is Love! Love is what we truly are. Not only that, but *only Love is real*.[11] Ta-da! That is the essential lesson to understand while we are here on this spinning sphere. If we all really remembered that delicious morsel of truth, we wouldn't need to read, or seek, or actively meditate—and definitely not suffer—anymore. Ever. In fact, we probably wouldn't even need bodies. We could just vibrate as the pure energy of our own true Love.

---

11 This is a *big* message in *A Course in Miracles.*

However, if you are reading these words, I assume that, like me, you are perhaps finding the way back to pure Love energy (though you may not use those exact terms). You may still hold certain beliefs that block your view of your own innate perfection. In that case, please continue.

I'm not sure why, but these days we seem to spend more time deleting junk e-mail or finding the perfect shoes than we devote to actively re-membering/pursuing/creating Love (unless we are falling in it—at which point it's darn hard to think about anything else). It's no wonder we don't remember much about Love! Despite our temporary Lovenesia, however, Love remains the power that moves us, and we really bless ourselves when we practice remembering it more. Our world would be perceived as beauty and peace and gladness if we could relearn to Love as often, as deeply, as consciously, and as creatively as possible.

Are you thinking I'm crazy right about now? A little too woo-woo "out there" to be believable? Well, what *is* "normal," then? Is it rushing around all day, feeling frustrated by our jobs/spouses/neighbors, listening to news of fiscal crises and wars, working hard and still not getting "there"? I con-tend that we've misidentified "normal" due to the ubiquity of *really* crazy stuff! If you ask me, the nightly news is crazy! Living on a planet where people kill each other on purpose is crazy! Hating folks for their beliefs or lifestyles is crazy! What I am suggesting here, "crazy" as it may sound, is to redefine "normal" to include big heaps of normal, everywhen[12] Love.

"And just how do I do that in all my spare time, Kelly?" you may be asking at this very moment. Glad you asked. It's so much easier than you expect because you can actually start every morning when you wake up—you don't even have to get out of bed! And here's still better news: you don't have to change anyone else, either. In fact, you have probably already experienced the frustration that attends any efforts to change

---

12 Isn't that such a great word? "Everywhen" was brought to us by that totally fabulous math geek and teacher of Albert Einstein, Hermann Minkowski. Thanks, Hermann!

someone else. It's always better to attempt to change what we have control over, like our perspective. No matter how hard we try (and believe me, I've spent way too much time trying), we just can't change anyone else! Simply begin by changing the way *you* treat *your* life. Everything else will change from that.

> **Seek not to change the world,**
> **but choose to change your mind**
> **about the world.**
>
> —*A Course in Miracles*,
> T-21.Intro 1:7

We can, if we choose, consciously begin our day thinking of all the people and things to Love. Imagine a Wednesday that began with looking at your partner, your children (even if they are far away, there are pictures), your dog, your pet boa constrictor, the sky, the water that comes out of the shower head, your cup of coffee, the plants on your windowsill, the teeth you get to brush, the birds singing optimistically, as if they have nothing better to do than fill up the mornings with music... and just feel the Love and gratitude. *There are so many things to Love!*[13] Every minute of every day, we can fill our minds and hearts with samples of Love.

If we decide to, that is. The choice is always our own.

---

13 Even if you currently seem to notice so many things going "wrong" in your life, you can start by finding gratitude for being "on this side of the dirt," as my funny dad says!

However, most of us start by lighting up some "electronical" (as my younger son calls them) for a dose of "reality," or opening our local paper to be "good citizens." We shower, floss, caffeinate, blow-dry, dash to work or school, and by 9:00 a.m. have done "ten thousand things," as Lao Tse would say, but not really Loved.

How much better to start the morning with Love than with the daily news! (I promise: the earth will still rotate on its axis if we remain ignorant of the current price of Apple stock or details of the latest bombing.) Imagine the feelings of delight that could pop up from those first "repentant thoughts" of the day. On days I begin with a little blessing-counting exercise, I am far more likely to assume the lead role in my own happy morning—and subsequent day. The alternative, a day begun unconsciously (in which I have, sadly, participated more often than I can count) can frequently involve stressing over lost library books, bad drivers, painters not showing up for the third day in a row, shoes left behind (sometimes all the above), or any number of trivialities. My family can tell and will always respond to my different energy—not in a good way.

⟨⟩

Love many things, for therein lies the true strength,
and whosoever loves much performs much,
and can accomplish much,
and what is done in love is done well.

—Vincent van Gogh

⟨⟩

I recently discovered that a sweet friend of mine, Sondra, already does this on a regular basis. With a smile on her face, she told me, "I had to get really big bonks on the head before I understood the importance of being grateful. But now I definitely get it, so I make sure to start out each day with gratitude. Gratitude precedes joy, not the other way around." The "bonks" she refers to were the painful loss of her accomplished husband to brain cancer, and her own serious experience of breast cancer a year later. Her brilliant focus not only makes *her* life happier, but the example she is setting for her darling children and lucky friends is profound. As Arnold Patent, inspiring author and truth sharer says, "What you focus on expands." Why not expand Love and gratitude into every moment we are here?

EXERCISE 1. A Really New Dawn

GO FOR IT!

Wake up about four minutes early, find a comfortable spot, and give this exercise a shot (or, alternatively, stay lounging in your snuggly, warm bed to do this exercise—you will still feel the results, as long as you don't fall back to sleep—and maybe even if you do return to Zzzzzz land!). Love and gratefulness feel very similar to me vibrationally, so see where your intuition takes you. When I practice this exercise, it makes a *huge* difference in my own "reality." Try it for a few days, and I know you will be surprised at the changes you experience. You may never turn on the news as a day starter again!

1. Set your timer for three minutes.[14] (I like to use the harp chime on my phone.)
2. Close your eyes, and take in several deep, rejuvenating breaths.

---

14 A timer, Kelly? But didn't you *just* purport that time doesn't exist? Well, yes, and while I don't believe in time as a linear, sequential phenomenon, clocks and timers do come in handy for now as "resting" tools. A timer keeps us from having to wonder if "quiet time" is up and get distracted from the delicious focusing and releasing at hand.

3. Start thinking of all the things you have to be grateful for, and delight in the *feelings* these thoughts incur. Anything and everything great you can conjure up is appropriate and welcome. Last night's view from your kitchen window of neighborhood kids playing basketball. The hilarious joke your oldest son told you. The Meyer lemon blossoms in your backyard. Your raise. Your child's upcoming piano recital. The delicious tiramisu your beautiful Italian friend shared with you. The start of football season. Anything that delights you!

4. When the timer rings (you will be surprised at how speedily those few minutes whizzed by), jot down your feelings, even if you can find only the back of a magazine and a broken crayon.

5. Repeat daily and be impressed by how your thoughts are shifting and how your energy is shifting. People will start smiling at you more, which will make you smile even more, which will make other people smile...you see how this can go!

Even if you don't practice this Love exercise in the morning, it's never too late to invoke Love's potency. If things get brambly one day, you can always to do a little ex post facto reveling in the power of Love. Late proves better than absolutely never. As an example...

For one birthday, my sweet husband planned the most wonderful trip for two to New York City. He scored amazing symphony and Broadway tickets and researched the dreamiest new romantic restaurants. This rare just-us weekend was going to be perfect. (Can you feel where this extra-large pile of expectations is headed?) Have I mentioned that we do battle about once every 8.93 years? (We definitely don't always agree on everything, but our disagreements seldom escalate to a notable level anymore.)

Oh, was Friday night fabulous: the French meal was *trés magnifique*, and the show was bust-a-gut hilarious. The entire evening, we indulged in full-sentence conversations (something our well-practiced children expertly thwart) and delighted in each other's company. We even slept in on Saturday, yet another luxury seldom afforded us by our darling offspring and their ceaseless activities.

Then came lunchtime. You'd think in a city famous for food, that perfect dining spot could have been easily found...yet "perfect" eluded us. The details of our rapid ascent up Mount Furious aren't important— though the speed with which we reached the apex was certainly extraordinary! Before our growling bellies could rein us in, we were standing on the streets of New York City, *yelling at each other*!

Shamefully (as if the stentorian outrage weren't vulgar and unworthy enough), the fight didn't end when the words stopped. Bolstered by hurt feelings, mangled pride, and a serious dose of indignation, the shadow of our monstrous altercation dogged us through the rest of our trip. We even brought it back on the airplane: large though it was, it hunkered down right between us!

Feeling increasingly uncomfortable with the weight of the beast at home with us, I asked my husband if we could consciously put Love in the middle, to see if that might help. This was an out-of-the-blue idea, but he was miserable, too, so he quickly agreed. While neither of us really knew the best way to proceed, we simply sat down facing each other, envisioning Love flowing to and from each other's heart. (Initially, we tried to do it with our eyes open, but we felt too silly and started giggling, so we closed our eyes and continued.) After a few minutes, we looked at each other and somehow agreed that we were done. *Immediately*, we both felt startlingly, spectacularly freed! The anger had completely melted away, as if it had never existed. When we each opened our eyes and got up after just minutes of Love sending, the beast had evaporated.

Now, *that* was a Love miracle.

I know *now* that we could have called on Love to solve things earlier, but our attachments to being "right" or "wronged," or whatever, kept us fending off joy with a vengeance for more than thirty-six hours! Hmmm, and peace was so easy to find once we finally "repented." Rumi was right when he said, "Your task is not to seek for love, but merely to seek and find all the barriers within yourself that you have built against it."

I realize this episode might look like a "little" miracle. A single husband-and-wife fracas in the middle of a world teeming with turmoil seems almost insignificant. But none of history's wars ever popped up full-grown. The hate virus requires tending. War is just the ultimate intensification of anger's untempered howls. *Left unstewarded, anger, resentment, fear, frustration—any form non-Love takes—can grow into all sorts of warfare, internal and external.* Thankfully, though, the more we invite Love into our lives and practice consciously Loving—removing our attention from non-Love—the more Love will flourish in and around us...and the happier we will be. A fabulous side effect of this practice is that those around us will also, by default, be happier...not because of anything we tell them, but because of how our own joy resonates with them. The goal here is to focus—always—on our own thinking and our own deeds.

So, ironically, most family members make *excellent* "Love target practice," serving, as they often do, as our first line of attack in the frustration department. Oddly, because I am so infinitely nutty about them, my children call on my equanimity reserves more than others. This fact makes them incredible and constant Love teachers for me. And not only do they give me the chance to practice unconditional Love (always good to practice!), but my connection to them helps me immediately feel Love's benefits. Following is another example of Love's conquering capacity, similar in its simple conclusion, though not nearly as dramatic as my regrettable Manhattan Madness.

Our youngest son is named Will (not William), and since his earliest days, he has been intent on living up to his name. Willful, Will of steel, iron-Willed, and so on, have all fairly represented his style and intensity. So, frequently, in convincing him to accede to plans other than his own, he staunchly champions his title. Such was the case with piano. For more time than I like to admit, the keyboard caused tears, frustration, and general vexation on both sides...that is, until we invoked the sending-Love technique.

One day, before the dreaded piano practice, I said, "Remember that time I was sending you Love, and you told me you saw green light coming from my heart to yours?"

"Yes," he answered honestly, not aware that this line of questioning was headed in a musical direction.

"Well, how about if we send that kind of Love to each other before we practice the piano? We'll see if it helps us have happier practices." He is so accustomed to experiencing relief from energy being sent his direction that he agreed right away. As with my husband, we directed Love to each other's heart, intending to make music fun again. Happily, the piano practice that followed was wonderful, as was almost every practice following. Note to self: if we feel the tug of less-than-funness, we just need to reengage our Loving intentions, and that can solve everything!

EXERCISE 2: Love Melt

GO FOR IT!

I recently had a conversation with a quite intelligent, creative gentleman who insisted that Love is not a "real" force. He went on to pronounce that science, however, is "real." (Curiously, he saw them at odds, science[15] and Love!) I'd gone down the oh-let-me-explain path before I realized I was on it (why do I still get caught in ego traffic?), so as soon as I did, I hopped off. No sense trying to *convince* someone of the power of Love! Better to *intentionally feel* it for ourselves and then just radiate it.

The following exercise is one way to actively, internally sense the energy of Love. Again, measuring devices are superfluous... you will *know* it. Of course, we have all felt Love at some point—hopefully, many points—in our lives, so this little three-minute activity may seem more like reheating than baking from scratch. It is very easy, and it has changed my life in wildly wonderful ways.

1. Think of how you are feeling at this very moment. Happy? Sad? Mad? Giddy? Just note it.
2. Stand or sit facing your partner, your child, or anyone willing! (You do not need to have something negative happening in your vibration to make this process interesting, or valuable, or surprisingly delightful, though the "before and after" might be more noticeable to you.) Make sure you are physically comfortable so you can bask in Love instead of having to focus on a foot that's falling asleep.
3. Hold the thought of extending Love in your mind. Now convert the *intention* of Love in your head to a *feeling* in your heart. Let everything "drop" from your head to the level of your heart. Really feel it.
4. Start your timer for three minutes of Love.
5. With your eyes open or closed (it doesn't matter; just do what feels best for you), begin imagining Love going from your heart to his or hers and back again. I like to connect my heart to someone with an infinity loop pattern.

---

15   And my guess is that what we now call "science" will be something else completely in years to come.

6. When the timer chimes, note how you feel. How does the sendee feel? (Writing it down is always a great way to go: that way you will remember better later.)
7. Enjoy the shift in energy!

There is no right or wrong way to practice the exercise above. Not only will every person experience something different, but each time *you* practice Love sending, your mileage may vary. In addition, even if you don't feel anything right away, the effects will show up later, in unexpected ways. Just be open to them.

To confirm that "right" and "wrong" aren't pertinent whatsoever to Love sending, I'm including a small sampling of responses from people who have kindly documented their Love sending exercises to remind us that it's all good. (Names have been changed to ensure that friends won't randomly hear their story on *Ellen!*)

Sven and Lulu

Sven wrote, "I wanted to do it with our eyes open, but Lulu preferred eyes shut. That probably speaks more to our relative attractiveness. We ended up doing it eyes open, and we each recorded our thoughts immediately afterward for research purposes. Please find our experiences below."

Sven: I love looking at her face. She is so beautiful. It reminds me how much I love her and all the good times we have shared. Like in Pebble Beach—that was magical. The ocean, the fresh air, spending time together, the golf. I only wish I had played a little better. I just wasn't hitting my driver all that great. I kept fading everything. I must be coming over the top on my downswing. Remember what that one guy told me a few years back about keeping my right elbow in? I'll bet that would fix it! I can't wait to try it. I probably have time to get to the driving range before dinner. Has it been three minutes yet?

Lulu: Oh, this is the coolest idea ever. I love Kelly. I love looking at my husband. I can tell he loves me just by the way he is looking at me. This is wonderful; we need to do it more often. Wait a minute, why is he looking at me like that? It's probably my eyeliner; I knew I should have gone with the lighter shade. I told that lady at the makeup counter, but, oh no, she knew best. OK, now he is smiling and has a spark in his eye. I'll bet he is thinking about us making love. That's when we are truly the closest. Uh-oh, I hope he doesn't expect that to happen now. I'm tired, and I need to cook dinner. What should we have for a vegetable? I need to get that damned oven fixed. Has it been three minutes yet?

Now let me introduce you to the couple who did the exercise in the car on the way home from a vacation! How nice of them to demonstrate that we don't have to stop living our normal lives to incorporate conscious Love. Love need never wait.

Cosmo and Sophia

Cosmo (before doing the Love Melt together): Anxious about work and a little bored being in the car.

Cosmo (after): We had been making drip castles on the beach, so I imagined dripping or drizzling love on Sophia so she always experiences it, not necessarily a deluge all at one time. I forced myself to focus on that and not work.

Sophia (before): Slightly anxious about the PTA seminar I will be attending, yet relaxed about the fun weekend we just had.

Sophia (after): Definitely feeling the Love loop with my honey. With my eyes closed, I rewatched him "pack-mule" all the crap to the beach and then back again for just two days. He does all of this because he loves me. I definitely forgot about PTA and spent time laughing because he *really* wants to leave most of the crap in the room!

I am including the next response as a Love "stretch goal." I am fortunate enough to know the couple who wrote it, and for them, the concept of actively stopping to *think* about including Love is a novelty because Love permeates their lives without having to be specifically invited. It is the place I hope we can all find ourselves—sooner, rather than later!

Clarence: When I described the three-minute exercise to my wife, she responded, "Isn't that essentially what we do all the time?" We went ahead and tried the exercise, and afterward we felt more in touch with the underlying, fundamental layer of our Love.

A Few Love-Sending Disclaimers

Everyone Wanders

Perhaps you have read that funny children's classic *Everyone Poops*, first published in Japan in 1977. I love it because it is such a lighthearted way to demystify an apparently hilarious yet perfectly natural act. Somehow, just acknowledging the obvious reduces its power to distract or embarrass us (this is true about more than poop, of course). It turns out, pooping and mind wandering have in common their complete ubiquity: everyone poops *and* mind-wanders. You probably know exactly what I mean. (Sven and Lulu know!). There you are, trying to focus—even for as few as three minutes—and suddenly, your to-do list commandeers every neuron that's ever synapsed in your cerebral cortex. Maybe you can't stop perseverating on Friday's board meeting. Or the plane reservation you need to change before the price goes up. Did you lock the front door?

At the risk of taking this analogy too darn far, I will highlight that the more you force, the harder you make things on yourself. (My insightful mother has always said, "Force creates resistance.") So when you begin your three minutes—resolute in Love thoughts toward your husband, child, boss, or the guy who just cut you off *and* gave you the finger—but find yourself pondering your golf swing or grocery list, just smile and bring yourself gently back. Think of it as a form of muscle building: buffing up your repenting muscle. *Every time we remind ourselves to focus on Love, our strength, abilities, and deep memory of it will increase.* Before you know it, you will think, "How funny that I used to set my timer to feel this way!"

Any Format Will Work

I think it's important to remember—and Sophia and Cosmo are perfect illustrations—that Love doesn't demand a specific proscribed way to be. Those divine Kodak moments seldom show up when we are poised with the camera in our hand. By having the attention and awareness that we want to create more Love experiences in our life, we will draw them to us. Don't be surprised, then, when you realize you've had a profoundly Love-filled encounter with the cashier at the paint store, or when you are stunned by the beauty of a rose blooming in your backyard, or even just being by yourself in a moment of silence.

Piglet: How do you spell "love"?
Pooh: You don't spell it…you feel it.

—A. A. Milne

IT'S NOTHING PERSONAL

When it comes to sending Love, I should state that ultimately, Love is not "personal." This may sound counterintuitive—and not even very nice—but hang with me here. Of course, right now it's easier to send Love to people we know, or situations about which we can relate personally. But Big Love is for all, whether we know them, Love them, feel for them, or not. So, while sending Love to individuals or situations is a beautiful way to start living more Love, my personal goal is to Love impersonally. Maybe a better way to say it is that I hope to Love everyone equally. It does not mean I will Love my children, husband, extended family, friends, and others I consider close any *less*. No, far from that! *Someday I hope to Love everyone—including my kids, husband, family, and friends—so very, very much more, and with so much depth, that there is no distinguishing Love from itself.*

So I practice on strangers.[16]

Many years ago, when I first started experimenting with how consciously directed Love could affect situations, I was curious to see if it would have a noticeable impact on people with whom I had no blatant "connection." So while at a conference for all things organic, I began sending Love to booth-manning strangers. In my head, while talking to them about the benefits of, say, non-GMO soy, or pesticide-free baby food, I would hold the thought, "I Love you," and try to match it with a feeling of Love. Looking straight into their never-met-'em-before eyes, I'd repeat the intention of Love being directed at them, over and over.

Because this was my initial overt experiment with a specific form of Love sending, the responses surprised me. Everyone acknowledged the energy shift at some level, whether it was to smile more, offer me some

---

16 OK, so practicing on strangers isn't taking all-dimensional Love to the completely "impersonal level," but it feels like a directionally correct next step.

treats, or physically move closer during a conversation. But one young man stood out. I believe he was enlightening me on composting. We'd been chatting a couple of minutes when he had to stop, unable to finish his insights about rotting vegetables, and blurt out, "You are so beautiful!" Now, I was already an old lady by then, and his voice/demeanor had nothing at all to do with what I physically looked like. He was responding to the energy he felt, and "beauty" was his way of interpreting that Love.

⌒⟶

**Believe in a love that is being stored up for you
like an inheritance, and have faith that in this love
there is a strength and a blessing so large
that you can travel as far as you wish without
having to step outside it.**

—RAINER MARIA RILKE

⌒⟶

Just imagine what could happen if you regularly directed silent Love to your fourteen-year-old daughter. Or your shy neighbor. Or the barista who regularly fixes you your cup of get-up-and-go. (Your dog probably sends you unconditional Love all the time, and it feels great, doesn't it?)

The Love we truly are is waiting for us to think about it and remember it. *Love is the most real thing about us, and it is what connects and blesses us all.* A beautiful American novelist and poet, Aberjhani, calls Love "our most unifying and empowering common spiritual denominator." Amen!

CHAPTER 3

Miraculosity and Bliss: The New Normal

Miracles are like pimples, because once you start looking
for them, you'll find more than you ever imagined possible.

—LEMONY SNICKET

It's not miracles that generate faith,
but faith that generates miracles.

—FYODOR DOSTOYEVSKY

I LAUGHED OUT LOUD WHEN I saw a sign proclaiming, "'Normal' is just a setting on my dishwasher." That is certainly true in our house, with an important twist: there are actually *two* things I call "normal." One is the dishwashing option; the other is "miraculosity," or the state of living in miracles.

Except for my dishwasher, normal wasn't always that way. *I didn't know for a true fact that I could tap into a happier life by switching my intention to a new setting—by changing my mind.* Applying purposeful intention, I learned to step into a less stressful, new-and-improved way of being in the world (most of the time, anyway).[17]

It's a bit hard to describe, so foreign is it to our present ways, but it minimally involves waking up happy and smiling for no specific reason. Worries fall away. "Happy coincidences" abound. It's bliss. One woman likened this state to an old-fashioned Disney movie, where birds sing happily all around the animated leading lady, and little animals scurry forth to help with whatever needs to be done. In this scenario, though, there's no evil witch.

Miraculosity is what I experience personally more and more, and it is true for many, many people. As is perfectly obvious by the planet's present day state of affairs, however, it is not what most humans presume true and, therefore, experience. *Believing in miraculosity makes it even more available to us.* Insisting otherwise will instruct our electrobiochemistry to confirm a less delightful "true fact" of life.

Let's back up a tad to consider miracles and our experience of them. First, what *is* a miracle, really? We flippantly sling that word around, but I wonder how often the idea of a "miracle" is sincerely contemplated as it relates to our life experiences. For example, if you were living in Rome with centurions for neighbors, and someone pressed a ringing cell phone in your hands, you'd probably scream. When you got over your shock, you would probably call that little box a miracle. These days, if it were the last shopping day before Christmas, and you snagged the parking place closest to your favorite store—in the rain—you might deem that a miracle. And what about an airplane landing without a wing, or a spontaneous healing during a Wednesday-night prayer group?

---

17 I do not mean to say that I live in bliss every moment of every day—not yet, that's for certain! But by bringing an awareness of Love's possibilities to my days, I find myself increasingly in miraculosity's neighborhood. In fact, writing this book has become a chance for me to "focus my focus," and during this process, I have found myself even more regularly on a happiness high!

To many, a "miracle" is something that can't be scientifically or logically explained (like an iPhone would have been a few centuries ago). For me, miracles are time-independent phenomena that call forth the vibration of Love. *It's not the* **what** *that matters; it's the* **how**. A miracle swaps fear for Love, heals what seems sick, and lightens what seems heavy. Miracles help us find our way to the truth about ourselves (which definitely has everything to do with Love).

A majorly important book on the topic that takes me new places each time I open its tattered binding, or read it on my phone, *A Course in Miracles*,[18] puts it like this:

> Miracles occur naturally as expressions of love. The real miracle is the love that inspires them. In this sense, everything that comes from love is a miracle.[19]

So, if miracles can "occur naturally" through something as ubiquitous and accessible as Love, couldn't we expect miracles to be part of our dailyness? *Why not believe in miracles, create them, invite them for dinner, and offer them a place to stay every single day? Just because we have not doesn't mean we cannot.* From this perspective, modern miracles seem not so elusive, and, in fact, potentially everywhere. Really, then, it goes back to changing our minds—repenting—about their possibilities as the sine qua non for most of us to become miracle-experiencing regulars.

---

18 OK, "book" seems a bit disrespectful to describe this three-volume, life-upgrading opus of insight. That's kind of like saying Beethoven wrote some OK music. *A Course in Miracles* (*ACIM*) is more like a full-scale "do-over" of our thinking. It includes a set of lessons to practice, a text (the first time I read a page, I had to look carefully to be sure I hadn't been attempting the Swahili version—really, I didn't understand a word!), and a manual for teachers. I will refer to *ACIM* frequently because it has been an incredibly powerful source of wisdom for me.

19 *A Course in Miracles*, T-1.I.3:1-3.

Kelly Corbet

For a long time now, though, we've treated miracles like the good china…too special for just a Thursday. We don't balk much about ancient miracles pulled off by the likes of the Buddha, Jesus, and other spiritual luminaries, but seriously, who would even *attempt* to part a sea these days? And if creating bread and fish out of thin air or walking on water are really available to us (the Buddha and Jesus are *both* reported to have water walked), why do almost 870 million humans on this planet seem to suffer from "chronic undernourishment"?[20]

Like I said, I'm pretty sure it has to do with temporarily forgetting our innate perfection, our connection to Love, and our true source. But let me share some really great news: now (this very instant) is the perfect time to start remembering! We can recall that miracles are our truth, and hence accelerate their inclination to show up for us. In fact, *rediscovering our own miraculousness is the most important, valuable, world-peacing, beauty-spreading, kind, and generous thing we can do.*

A good step in returning to our miraculous true selves, is to aim at *feeling* the Love we are. The following is a surprisingly simple way to experience the feeling of Love in our own bodies. Think of it as a Miracles Fast Pass. I won't give you the punch line in advance, but if you are like most people, you will feel it immediately and probably be very surprised.

EXERCISE 3: The Bob

GO FOR IT!

1. Stand with your eyes closed in a place relatively chaos-free. (If that kind of space is unavailable to you, don't worry;

---

20 This number is from data collected between 2010 and 2012, according to the UN Food and Agriculture Organization.

28

this exercise can be accomplished just as effectively in the middle of Calcutta or Shinjuku Station.)

2. Breathe in. Breathe out. Repeat this calm, conscious breathing pattern a few times while you "drop" into your heart space.
3. Think of Love. Fill your chest with it. Expand that feeling beyond your body. Think of people and things you Love. Imagine your happiest moments.
4. Notice what is happening in your body. Is it moving in any direction? Is it shifting noticeably?
5. Now think of yucky, hateful stuff. (I know, not nearly as much fun.) Conjure up Hitler or war or abused puppies.
6. What is happening to your body now?
7. Take in a few more breaths, and remember the Love feeling.

I call this exercise the Bob because people generally either bob up and down or to the front and back of their center. In any case, bodies generally, unexpectedly, move. The typical trend of this deceptively simple practice is that folks will go forward or "up" when tapping into Love, as if being drawn in, or lifted. I generally categorize Love's "opposite" as fear.[21] (It shows up in such a variety of flavors—hate, anger, violence, greed, jealousy—but fear is at its base.) It immediately pushes people "away," or down. When my data-loving, super-smart oldest son good-heartedly attempted this the first time, his eyes almost popped out of his head in complete disbelief over "the bob" his body carried out, oblivious to his conscious intention.

So why does that happen? *By aligning with the vibration of Love, we are beckoned forward. Invoking Love's opposite sets us back.* Literally.

---

21 OK, Love doesn't really have an opposite, but for the sake of illustration…

This isn't too far off from what you have probably experienced yourself. Think about happy people. Aren't you "drawn to" them? And can't you just feel your resistance, or inclination to keep your distance from folks in whom you perceive a "bad vibe"? You've actually already done the Bob on hundreds of occasions; it's just that this time, you were bobbing consciously.

Now, imagine you do the Bob daily, hourly—every minute—because, in fact, you do. The question is just how to do the Bob with your conscious intention to draw in more Love, fun, joy, happy people, and awesome experiences—miracles.

So, as I will continue to reiterate (and reiterate, and reiterate…), your mindful awareness of miracles' ubiquity will change your relationship to them. In the past, you may have relegated miracles to religious-only phenomena, like Christmas Eve tales or the *nes* (Hebrew for "miracle") of a day's worth of oil going strong for eight days; events that bring big, noticeable smiles, like the birth of a child, or winning a cruise. But now that you can start to feel your way closer to miraculosity, you have the opportunity to experience things from a new angle. *A different—conscious— expectation will create a different—conscious—result.*

Miracles aren't necessarily grandiose. Their simplicity, their accessibility, their everydayness is really part of their power. For example, getting kids ready for school in the morning, a daily activity, was once angst-filled and helter-skelter in our house, no matter how well I thought I had prepared the night before. Now, overarchingly, weekday preparations flow smoothly. Kids empty the dishwasher without having to be asked 9,387 times, teeth get brushed (mostly…and even if they don't, it somehow doesn't seem to matter so much anymore), and shoes get found (again, mostly). All that feels blissful, miraculous. So please don't believe for a femtosecond that miracles are just for "big stuff" (although there were times that not being able to find shoes before school seemed very, very,

very big!). What seems *big* now is the general joy that usually accompanies us to school these days.

In fact, as you practice invoking miracles through Love, you will be able to watch miracles arise in the humblest of moments and involve the very plainest of elements. I can hardly think of a more beautiful example than the one Nancy Singleton Hachisu, an inspirational cook and culture sharer, wrote about so beautifully in her delicious book *Japanese Farm Food*. Overtly, it is about rice, but it's not *really* about rice.[22]

ON WASHING RICE

Cooking is one of the most soothingly therapeutic occupations we can do when not hurried. But so often our minds are elsewhere as we go through the motions, not thinking of the food in front of us that we are chopping or stirring into yet another meal. I notice my cooking students mixing dough completely disengaged from what they are doing, chatting across the counter with other students equally distracted from their tasks. They are often completely unaware of what is happening in the bowl before them. Now, I counsel, pour yourself into the bowl and put your love in the food. Use a light hand with a powerful spirit.

It used to be that our teenage son, Andrew, was in charge of washing the rice—a task he performed with a singular lack of enthusiasm. But one day, a few years ago, Takaaki [Nancy's husband] and the boys were off doing pottery, so I made the rice. Andrew and I share a common trait: we both tend toward the slapdash. When under the gun, my cooking usually involves a lot

---

22 Roy Choi, in his interesting book *LA Son: My Life, My City, My Food*, also writes Zenishly about what seems to be rice washing, but is really so much more: "Wash your rice to cleanse, not to clean...transferring all your energy to the rice as the rice transfers its own energy to you...Get deeper with it."

of swearing, spilling, and blood. I'm no less focused, but "in the zone," so stay out of my way. It's dangerous…

With a singular lack of enthusiasm, I went out to our dusty storage house…and scooped out some rice from a 25-kilogram sack. I brought the rice into the house and set about washing it. I felt the grains bounce off my hand as I scrubbed them. The cool water slipped against the grains and through my fingers as the rice sent soft little currents up my arm. I thought about how those grains got to be in my sink. I remembered planting that very rice by hand the year before—squelching around in the mud. I thought about the work it takes to grow each grain of rice. And I felt the energy that my farmer husband had put in, helped along the way by the sun, soil, and water. I felt how beautiful each little grain was—so simple and perfect, but so hard to produce. Each little grain so precious.

And that night when Tadaaki took his first bite of rice, his eyes widened in surprise, and he asked me what I had done to make the rice taste so good. What had been my special touch? I told him I had put love into it.[23]

Given that our current belief system asserts "reality's" solidity, this rice transformation may sound a bit odd, if not plain bonkers—particularly if you are new to miracle making. But with her Love, Nancy Singleton Hachisu actually changed the quality of the rice and brought miracles to her dinner table served in a bowl! Just imagine how great *every day* would be if we did precisely that (and included breakfast and lunch Love!).

Now then, if we can improve the taste of rice—so seemingly inert—with Love, the possibilities for improving interactions with our fellow

---

23 This is only one of many wonderful insights from Nancy's *Japanese Farm Food*, published by Andrews McNeal Publishing, LLC, in 2012, p. 140.

humans are wildly colossal. Just as the rice didn't need to "do" anything to vibrate at a more delicious frequency, neither do other people need to be "actively involved" in *you* changing *your* perception of their wonderfulness or your own. For example, say your partner or your very teenagery teenager (those two categories of folk seem consistently at the top of everyone's "most complained about" list) is driving you to the crazy. What have you been likely to do in the past? Probably discuss "the problem" with friends, coworkers, your sister, the dry cleaner, your cat. But how the heck is that type of cavil going to *solve* the problem? It cannot. I know from experience.

Yes, I'm aware people tell themselves and each other that sharing this information helps "get it off my chest." And I'd have to be living in the Oort cloud not to realize the profusion of spouse gripes in our culture—as if voicing complaints to everyone *but* the person in question could actually help. *However,* whah-whah-whahing just builds a matrix of energy around the thing/behavior we already don't want! Going one step further, I believe that often, even voicing the irritations to the irritant directly may not be the best answer. (I didn't say "always," so put any defenses that sentence may have caused back in the drawer, please.) Looking at it from a presume-it/project-it energetic perspective, *griping grows the grief* (remember Heisenberg's Observer Principle; it tells us that observing/measuring something causes it to change).

*Suffering is how long and far
and wide we schlep
our challenges with us after they are over.*

It's all about our choice in the matter—whatever the matter. In *A Course in Miracles*, an early lesson radically suggests that we "let miracles replace all grievances,"[24] and that "each decision that you make is between a grievance and a miracle."[25] If miracles are all around us—and by now you know I believe they are—then looking past the stuff that bugs us, and directly to the Love being obscured by our attitude is the way to witness those miracles. I've found the following exercise to be a much better means to remember the awaiting miracle than kvetching about a particular human "thorn." It requires about the same amount of time as waiting for a burger at the drive-thru, and the results among testers have been spectacular.

EXERCISE 4: 3 x 3 (3 minutes x 3 participants: you, consciousness, and the recipient)

GO FOR IT!

This exercise, 3 x 3, is similar to the Love Melt in terms of intention, but it's even more powerful because the "recipient" doesn't have to be involved at any conscious level. Here's how to go 3 x 3–ing, miracle-style:

1. Think of someone who's really been getting your goat lately. I'll bet that person's name has already popped up for you, hasn't it? Now set aside three whole minutes to spend peacefully thinking about that person's good qualities. "Feel" something nice about her. (No being petty: we *all* have good qualities!)

2. Grab your timer, and for the next 180 seconds, think of things that person does that are really kind/valuable/delightful to you. This may involve some upfront reframing on your part. For example, rather than being mad that your husband shrunk your

---

24 *A Course in Miracles*, W-pI.78.1:1.
25 *A Course in Miracles*, W-pI.78.2:1.

he'd-never-guess-how-expensive-they-were yoga pants in the dryer, why not shift to considering how great it was of him to do the laundry?

3. Send that person Love and gratefulness for offering you the chance to see things from a completely new perspective. It's OK to wander; just return if you realize you were heading off point.

4. When your chime beckons you out of the happy thoughts, I'll bet you will be surprised at how quickly the time flew. More than that, you will have reoriented your viewpoint in a way that the negative thoughts will have a less easy route through your brain.

5. Repeat this for four days. When you wake up on day five, you'll be delighted!

One renewed woman reported, "Day two, and I already feel different. My hubby even looked cute when he picked me up at the airport!" (Note: that was a major shift from the previous week!)

I should probably make a serious disclaimer right about now. It may appear that I am tra-la-la-ing along, completely ignoring the idea that people can experience really tough lives. Lest you get your underwear in a tight little bundle that this way of thinking—that miracles are easier than we have expected or experienced so far, and that they are available to absolutely everyone—is insensitive to the planet's legions who do not even enjoy fresh water, the freedom to learn/believe what they want, or safety from physical harm, please know that I do not discount them in any way. In fact, they are the biggest reason I wrote this book. I believe we are all connected at the most fundamental level—in fact, we aren't even "separate" beings—so the "individual" I have not even met will not be truly free until each one of us is "free" to remember our true selves. Those folks I've never sat next to at dinner or met on the subway, *they are all me* (and you and us). I do not presume to know what complete connecting will look like, but I do know that extending Love—and therefore miracles—is the most potent way I can conceive to shift things for everyone. *Interconnectedness means that when we change our own minds for the better, we change everything for the better.* A different way of thinking creates a different way of manifesting life on the entire planet, not just for us as "individuals."

One of the most heartrending examples of this comes from the beautiful soul, Immaculée Ilibagiza, author of the incredibly profound *Left to Tell: Discovering God amidst the Rwandan Holocaust.* Calling her a Rwandan genocide victim would completely miss the point of the book. She is a miracle maker, a forgiveness maven, an inspiration, and a peace mentor, but she is no victim! Immaculée transformed an über-horrific situation into miraculosity—for herself *and* the world—because of the unique and powerful way she chose to think about her experience. Here's what she wrote:

> I knew that my heart and mind would always be tempted to feel anger—to find blame and hate. But I resolved that when the negative feelings came upon me, I wouldn't wait for them to grow or fester. I would always turn immediately to the Source of all true power: I would turn to God and let His love and forgiveness protect and save me.[26]

Now, if that's not "repenting" in the truest, original-Greek sense of the word, I don't know what is!

Somehow, most of us (not Immaculée Ilibagiza!) have come to believe that it's easier, or better, or more "appropriate" to harbor anger and hate than to Love and forgive. But *forgiveness not only helps the forgiver; it stops the current of animosity and vengeance.* Fortunately, you don't have to be locked in a tiny bathroom with seven other women for months, singed by war and its

---

26 Immaculée Ilibagiza and Steve Erwin, *Left to Tell: Discovering God amidst the Rwandan Holocaust* (Carlsbad, CA: Hay House, 2007).

concomitant chorus of screams and gunshots to really understand this. There are gentler reminders.

One sweet hint comes in the form of a famous Zen story about how we unthinkingly cart non-Love around with us. I read it first in Jon J. Muth's beautiful children's book *Zen Shorts*. It goes something like this:

STUCK IN THE MUD

Two monks were traveling along a muddy road, rain and puddles everywhere. Amid the muck, just in front of them, was a wealthy gal, halted by the downpour and her unwillingness to sully her beautiful silk kimono. Though monks were not supposed to touch females, the older one quickly picked her up and carried her across the way to less muckiness.

Without a word of thanks or kindness from the silk-clad maiden, the monks continued on their way. After quite a while, the younger monk couldn't bear the rudeness, the injustice, the disrespect of it all and proclaimed, "We aren't allowed to touch women *and* that chick was just a bag of bad manners! I can't believe how she treated you!"

The older monk very simply offered this in response: "My friend, I set her down miles ago and left her right there. Why are *you* still carrying her?"

If you do not consider this brief parable an example of a miracle, I must ask you, **What is conscious inner peace, if not miraculous?** A cursory survey of random people (watch folks as they drive their cars, or wait in line at the post office) will surely confirm that "happy and healthy" very successfully evade the title of "normal." The Mayo Clinic conducted a study, revealing that almost 70 percent of Americans are on at least one pharmaceutical drug (doesn't that seem like a stunningly high percentage to you?), with antidepressants being the second most popular type of pills being popped.[27]

Even in the face of those surprising statistics, I maintain that finding joy in the everyday *is* bliss, *is* miraculosity, and *is* totally rediscoverable by each of us. Lucky for us, miracles don't require a war or a holiday in their honor.

Now, subtlety is not a hallmark of our culture, nor am I prone to delicate understatement myself (my entire family can quickly confirm that), so the fact that inner peace can arrive modestly and trumpetless took me a while to recognize. I won't say bliss sneaks up on you, but it often can follow a trajectory similar to my plants when I feed them: I see improvement in magnitudes that feel inconsequential day over day, and *astounding* improvements week over week. That is exactly what has happens to me when I feed my belief in, receptivity to, and understanding of miracles.[28]

The more you practice the types of exercises in this little book, focusing consciously on Love, the more you will feel how astoundingly *you* are growing upward in inner peace and miraculosity. You will probably find yourself wanting to practice "feeling the Love" more and more—not so much to better your abilities to focus (though you definitely will), but because the exercises have such life-improving side effects! Before you know it, you will move onto "greater" miracles, beyond just "feeling constantly happy."

---

27 From "Nearly Seven in Ten Americans Take Prescription Drugs, Mayo Clinic, Olmsted Medical Center Find," June 2013, www.mayoclinic.org/2013-rst/7543.html. For the record, I have *nothing* against antidepressants because they can be very, very helpful. What I'm highlighting is the obvious: if we are finding our own keys to happiness, we will probably not be seeking them from the pharmacy.

28 That being said, let me not limit your possibility of *immediate* joyhood and miraculosity. Our general predisposition in the other direction, however, frequently suggests a more gradual crescendo. Feel free to buck the trend.

I should make this point before going on, though, because, as silly as it may sound, all miracles are really the same "size" (stay with me here; this amazing but true fact will help you reap more of them). I know miracles *seem* to come in different magnitudes—from an unaccountable remission of a painful disease to a good test grade or finding a diamond in the middle of a busy street. Actually, however, *miracles seem "big" only relative to our expectations. All miracles show up exactly the size of Love,* the girth of which is, of course, unmeasurable. What metric could we possibly use to judge where Big Love might stretch and spill and meander?

For example, healing physical illness seems to be a Big Miracle in most people's minds. Initially, I'd decided against including stories of "miraculous healings" here for a few reasons. But I changed my mind (which, after all, is the point of this whole book!). Hopefully it can be valuable and instructive to know the wildly varying ways that we can expect miracles to be naturally occurring. That includes "healing" what seems sick.

So I am sharing some "miraculous" healing stories, after all—not to show you what "I" can "do," but to illustrate that you can "do" these things, too![29] First I must tell you, though, that *a miracle, whether physical healing, fight stopping, piano practice easing, or any number of Love-generated improvements, is not "done" by anything more than reconnecting with Love and resonating at that frequency.* Miracles we perceive as healing, then, aren't so much "healing" as remembering who we really are, and seeing through remembering eyes. I don't "do" anything other than vibrate at the frequency of Love—something you've already, hopefully, experienced many times yourself—and the person who wants to feel better entrains to that frequency. Like a tuning fork. Simple as that.

---

29 I'm using all these darn quotes around words I find inaccurate, or inept; my apologies. As I mentioned before, words are just symbols of symbols and can only really point in the general direction. Such remains the case as I try to explain miraculosity and "healing."

Anyone can participate in the miracle of healing. It doesn't take any "special equipment" like a theology degree, crystals, divining rods, incense, candles, esoteric symbols, or a magic wand. It does, however, require faith. If you don't think you can access the power of Love, you will prove yourself correct.

Here's how I reconnected with what I'll call "healing energy," an energy we all can access in many different ways. I used to have a company called Smart Foods Healthy Kids. My goal was to teach parents and children how to eat in ways that nourished their brains and bodies. We worked with schools, individuals, and families; taught cooking classes; and spoke whenever and wherever possible. The Smart Foods Healthy Kids website was filled with videos and healthy recipes. I met a lot of wonderful people and was happy with numerous "microchanges" my little company helped engender. Yet almost every day, I felt disappointed. I was working harder and harder, and the statistics were only getting worse. National news thwacked that fact in my face every single day. I wasn't making a dent, and I wasn't even happy trying. I focused waaayyyy too much on foods I thought were healthy (and unhealthy) for my family (and pretty much everyone else), which was not easy on anybody. And I certainly wasn't much fun at a dinner party: I'm pretty sure my "good food/bad food" mentality made folks feel censured.

It was hard to accept how "wrong" it all felt. My mother has always said that when things are right, they are easy. Only on rare occasions did that business feel "easy." And it seldom felt "fun" (that should have been my biggest hint!). So, finally, finally, finally, I shut down Smart Foods Healthy Kids. It was a quite painful process in which I participated with the enthusiasm of a blobfish.

The day I filed for formal dissolution of my company, something very odd and wonderful happened: I could *feel* energy flowing out of my hands. What? I know. It was kind of unbelievable to me at the time, too. The only way I can describe it is that it felt like someone installed an invisible faucet on my palms and opened the spigot.

Unfamiliar with this feeling, I called my sweet neighbor and asked her to come help me test whatever was going on. Obligingly—because she is just the type to help at a moment's notice—she hustled on over. Because I'd previously experienced "energy work" while on a massage table, I asked her to stretch out. I suggested that we just see what might happen. Again, obligingly, because she is just the type, she flattened out as I turned the "faucet" on. I just swooshed my hands around the air above her and felt a "flow" from my palms. During the few minutes I was "air-spraying" Love energy over her, I "saw" (my eyes were closed) something that looked like lips but definitely made from "stomach material." The lips looked like they were trying to open up. Weirdly, I saw those unusual "lips" twice, so I sent them Love (I guess). I also thought I should mention them to my friend to see if they meant anything to her. I was definitely *not* expecting her response.

"That's my *cervix*, Kelly!" she acknowledged, wide-eyed. "I didn't want to say anything because I really don't like to complain, but tomorrow morning at five o'clock, I'm going in to have my cervix scraped. There were problems when I went in before, because things didn't open up enough."

Oh, those "lips out of stomach material" *were* a cervix, I realized. Certainly not what I had anticipated! I told her, "I get the impression it will go well. I felt like it wanted some Love directed its way, so I sent some. I *think*."

Since that day, I've experimented a lot with Love vibrating. People have been known to hobble to my house wearing a back brace and leave after just a few minutes of peacing-out at Love's frequency to attend a Zumba class. One talented friend, whose neck pain was causing trouble with her golf game, told me she felt just like a bobblehead after our energetic time together!

Most of the pain level decreases and "healings" I've witnessed are self-reported, which makes them seem somehow less valid than if medical statistics, or scientifically acceptable "proof," were backing them up. One summer, however, conveniently, as I was starting to write this book, two instances of documentability offered themselves up within a week of each other. One was with a beautiful woman, Karen, who I knew only as the mother of my son's friend, and the other miracle demonstration happened with one of my oldest and dearest soul sisters, Sue.

In the first situation, Karen—who has now become a friend—called me while I was in California to ask me for help with her thirteen-year-old's medical issues. Karen's son is a charming teenager with a good sense of humor, a kind heart, and type 1 diabetes. They had been informed of seriously elevated protein levels in his urine, which could lead to kidney damage, among other dangers. The nephrologist had recommended that her son take the hypertension medicine, Lysinopril, for the sake of his endangered kidneys. But taking the drug concerned Karen. Her intuition restrained her. And no wonder, according to the Mayo Clinic, here are just *a few* of the possible side effects from taking Lysinopril:

> Blurred vision, confusion, sweating, unusual tiredness or weakness, body aches, chest pain, chills, common cold, cough, diarrhea, difficulty breathing, fever, headache, vomiting, fast or irregular heartbeat, joint pain.

Though she has *nothing* against pharmaceutical help, it's not hard to imagine why Karen wanted to find an alternative to help her child. She called me, though we'd never even had a casual phone conversation before! What was especially surprising, however, as I later discovered, was that she'd had *no idea* I'd been participating in energetic health shifts with other people. She just listened to her intuition (she is really good at that). As she puts it, "I went with my gut feeling that the hypertension medication was not necessary and trusted the whispering that told me I could help through energy, love, light—whatever you want to call it." She then called to enlist me in the "whatever you want to call it" category.

Together we sent her son Love and light from different states and different time zones, but with one purpose: to help her son's body realign itself with its perfect wellness. We would speak with each other on the phone, hang up, and turn on our timers—sometimes for three or four minutes, sometimes for as many as ten minutes. We only "mediprayed," as she creatively calls it, for two or three weeks before it was time to head back to the nephrologist again.

At the doctor's office, the nurse documented Karen's confession that the recommended medicine had not been administered to her son. In the examination room, awaiting the doctor's arrival, Karen was nervous. However, the doctor came in smiling, informing her that when he saw the amazing numbers on her son's chart, he was about to self-congratulate for having prescribed such a fabulous solution. He was absolutely stunned to see that Karen had not given her son any kind of medicine. "I don't know what you did, but whatever it was, it worked!" He added, "I've never seen numbers like this without medication in my career!"

Now, I am *not* advocating everyone drop all pharmaceutical help and Love themselves to health. But please *do* know that health without drugs can be a possibility for many.[30]

The second medically notable example happened, coincidentally, the following week. My very close friend Sue, whose son, Luke, was best friends with my oldest son since before they could run, was telling me

---

30 A word about conventional medicine: I appreciate it greatly in my life! I am thankful for it! Were it not for conventional medicine, my darling heart-transplanted father wouldn't be here to tell me eye-rolling jokes and helping uncountable numbers of people, nor would my redheaded son have appeared on the planet. You will never hear me criticizing conventional medicine! I'm just saying that there are alternatives perhaps worth including—options that might actually suit us better in certain situations—if we open our minds to the possibilities and attend to our expectations.

about Luke's painful shoulder that required surgery. I'll let her tell the story in her own words:

Luke's Story
July 2013

Luke was a twelve-year-old boy who loved to play baseball. He had the most strikeouts of any other player in the league and routinely clocked a 65-mile-per-hour fastball. In the spring of 2013, he started experiencing severe pain in his right shoulder. During one game, he heard a "pop" in his shoulder and was unable to continue throwing the ball. In fact, he could not lift his right arm at all or have any pressure on his hand. When we left the field, I considered going straight to the emergency room but decided to give him an anti-inflammatory and put ice on his shoulder at home.

The following morning, he was still in considerable pain. So we scheduled an appointment with his pediatrician and were sent for an x-ray. The radiologist diagnosed him with a separated growth plate in his shoulder and recommended a follow-up with an MRI using contrast dye. The MRI, along with an examination from a pediatric orthopedic surgeon, rediagnosed him with a SLAP tear (a torn labrum tendon). This was not an uncommon injury for a baseball pitcher, but definitely an injury that required surgery and insertion of hardware.

We were referred to a highly regarded pediatric orthopedic surgeon. We decided to wait until the end of the school year for the surgery because recovery from that surgery is long and painful. The tendon is reattached to the bone with a clamp. The clamp is secured through small holes drilled through the shoulder bone. Recovery to normal activity for a child takes approximately eight weeks, with return to pitching somewhere between six and eight months.

My dear friend Kelly was visiting in June, shortly before the operation. I told her about Luke's condition and the pending surgery. She suggested doing energy work on Luke. I believed energy was helpful for thought and emotional conditions but did not think it could possibly change a physically torn tendon. After all, it was loose and flapping around in his shoulder—I had seen the medical proof of it, and two doctors had confirmed the problem— how would it reattach by being sent Love?

Well, I'm a Kelly fan, and she has helped me tremendously with panic attacks, so there was no way I was going to say no, although I really did *not* think it would work. I even reminded her, "The tendon is torn; I saw it on the MRI."

She responded, "I know," and I guess she didn't take that as the final word. So we did a couple of energy sessions, while the doctor went ahead with the scheduled procedure.

The day of the operation was scary for us. I was told that Luke would be in surgery for two hours. I settled into the lounge and prepared for the wait. Surprisingly, approximately forty-five minutes after my son was rolled into the operating room, the surgeon appeared in the waiting room to talk to me. I asked immediately if something was wrong. He said, "Well, kind of," and took a seat next to me with pictures of the inside of Luke's shoulder.

I was prepared for very bad news—why did he stop surgery to come out and talk to me? He said, "Luke does not have a torn labrum."

This was a shock: "OK, well, what does he have?" I asked.

"He has a frayed rotator cuff, but certainly not serious enough to require surgery." He seemed very embarrassed and said, "This is very unusual. I've never had this happen before." He had no explanation, however, of how two medical experts had seen something on an MRI that was not there.

Luke's arm was patched up, and we were sent home. I vacillated between anger and relief. Then I told Kelly the story. As I sat with her, I remembered that we had done energy work on Luke.

Trained and well-respected radiologists and pediatric surgeons read the very sophisticated MRI images. Their experience created absolutely no doubt that Luke had torn his labrum. Besides, all of Luke's physical symptoms supported the SLAP-tear diagnosis.

Something changed all that. I came to believe that as incredible as it was, Luke had been healed by directing Loving energy his way. The power of energy working at a cellular level cured my son. Kelly calls it "the power of Love."

I'm really, really thankful for Luke's improved shoulder, for decreased protein numbers, for canceled surgeries (Luke's has not been the only canceled operation), and so on. I am a believer! But sometimes things do not work out as I hope or intend. Sometimes, I don't know why, the results I can witness are not in line with my ideas of helping people return to their natural state of health. I've had to let go of my expectations (and the ego stuff around those expectations because, really, it's *not* about me) and deeply accept that there are things going on behind the scenes about which I have absolutely no clue. Whether I see the anticipated results immediately or not, I remain convinced that sending Love, or vibrating at that frequency, or whatever you want to call it, somehow brings our interpretation of the situation closer to the truth. Even if I don't know precisely how. Anyway, there's no downside to sending Love, and it makes *me* feel great every time I do it, so I am not deterred.[31]

Preparing for Miracles

As you dive more deeply into miracles, whether they are of a physical or emotional nature, I do have a miraculosity request: *do not be surprised when miracles start showing up regularly, repeatedly. By all means, be delighted, happy, respectful, grateful, humble, glorious, "repentant," and/or peaceful, but please do not be shocked.* After all, you aren't stunned when the sun comes up or when a dry little seed turns into a gorgeous flower…you see where I'm going. When something is natural, habitual, *expected*, it is not surprising. Miracles, therefore, should not shock us. How wonderful to finally remember that!

I mention this because for far too long, miracles have surprised me by showing up again and again. What I consciously invited in through the power of Love would appear, and I'd be dumbfounded pretty much every time. These days, I try to transform surprise into gratefulness, which is a far more appropriate response to something so clearly "in our nature." Like Dr. Wayne Dyer said, "I am realistic—I expect miracles."

---

31 It is very important for me to reiterate the fact that the "healings" have nothing to do with me, personally, unless *faith* is counted as part of the equation. The goal of this little book isn't to explain the how-to's of "healing" but to show you the various and delightful shapes miracles can take!

As I've mentioned, it's believing in miracles that gives them their power.[32] That great master of miraculosity, Jesus, said all it took for a miracle was a little, itsy bitsy speck of faith:

> Truly I say to you, if you have faith the size of a mustard seed, you will say to this mountain, "Move from here to there," and it will move; and nothing will be impossible to you.[33]

He didn't instruct us to pray for one hundred and seventy-two hours straight, slaughter a calf, and do the hokey-pokey. All he said was have a little faith. I believe he is telling us that *what we call "miracles" can be easily accomplished with nothing more than our real belief in them*. Expect and invite miracles in on a regular basis!

Miracles are a retelling in small letters of the very
same story which is written across the whole
world in letters too large
for some of us to see.

—C. S. Lewis

---

32 Actually, believing in *anything* strongly enough is exactly what gives it its power. The placebo effect wreaks havoc on the pharmaceutical industry! Placebo surgeries have even demonstrated improvement, illustrating how powerfully our thoughts control our perception of "physical reality."
33 Matthew 17:20.

WALT WHITMAN'S MIRACLES

Miracles

Why, who makes much of a miracle?
As to me, I know of nothing else but miracles,
Whether I walk the streets of Manhattan,
Or dart my sight over the roofs of houses toward the sky,
Or wade with naked feet along the beach, just in the edge of the water,
Or stand under trees in the woods,
Or talk by day with any one I love—or sleep in
the bed at night with any one I love,
Or sit at table at dinner with my mother,
Or look at strangers opposite me riding in the car,
Or watch honey-bees busy around the hive, of a summer forenoon,
Or animals feeding in the fields,
Or birds—or the wonderfulness of insects in the air,
Or the wonderfulness of the sun-down—
or of stars shining so quiet and bright,
Or the exquisite, delicate, thin curve of the new moon in spring;
These, with the rest, one and all, are to me miracles,
The whole referring—yet each distinct, and in its place.

To me, every hour of the light and dark is a miracle,
Every cubic inch of space is a miracle,
Every square yard of the surface of the earth is spread with the same,
Every foot of the interior swarms with the same;
Every spear of grass—the frames, limbs, organs, of men and women,
and all that concerns them,
All these to me are unspeakably perfect miracles.

To me the sea is a continual miracle;
The fishes that swim—the rocks—the motion of the waves
—the ships, with men in them,
What stranger miracles are there?"

—WALT WHITMAN, *LEAVES OF GRASS*

CHAPTER 4

What You Think, You See

⌒

We are shaped by our thoughts;
we become what we think.
When the mind is pure,
joy follows like a shadow that never leaves.

—*The Buddha*

PEOPLE HAVE ACCUSED ME OF living in La La Land. Like that's a bad thing, as if my insistence that *happiness is our natural state, and we remember it by connecting to our consciousness* is somehow at odds with "reality." So I gotta ask, "Whose reality?" Or, moreover, "What is 'reality'?"[34]

One would think that last question might be easier to answer, given that, *more than a century ago*, Ernest Rutherford—besides discovering the nucleus of the atom—learned that atoms are mostly empty space. Sure, we all learned that in grade school, right? Well, then, if atoms are mostly empty

---

34 All right, I confess: my ultimate view of reality doesn't include anything outside of myself. I tend to agree with Eddington and Jeans, two brilliant physicists without the PR gift of darlings like Einstein and, later, Feynman. That said, to get to the point of all that making sense, it's helpful to provide stepping-stones to the other side…I had to learn how to crack eggs before I could make an omelet.

space, and the "stuff" we see is made of atoms, what does that say about the "solid material" around us? So, again I gotta ask, "What is 'reality'?"

If reality is the still-clung-to Newtonian belief that the world is mechanistic, it's real only if it's visible and/or "solid," and it is absolutely predetermined by a set of rules that cold-shoulder consciousness, then La La Land seems like a giant step up! La La Land appears to include more creativity and fun, and less suffering and pain. Maybe such a concept isn't so ridiculous after all.

As a point of perspective, let's review just a few of history's screwball concepts about *reality*. Like the nutty one Nicolaus Copernicus offered up to replace geocentrism, the Middle Ages conviction that the earth was the center of the universe. Today, of course, you'd fail science class if you blurted out that planets all revolve around the earth, but back in the day, it was *fact*. Such a factual fact, in fact, that had he not the good fortune to croak soon after publishing *On the Revolutions of the Heavenly Bodies*, Copernicus may have faced censure similar to Galileo's for his like-minded heretical ideas.

Galileo, who also concluded that the earth circled the sun and not the other way around, added a special peevishness to his freethinking discoveries and wild beliefs by writing in Italian, rather than in Latin. That made his work far more popularly accessible and dangerous, according to church officials. The Roman Catholic Church famously condemned Galileo's work, offering him the choice to renounce his antagonistic ideas or experience torture Inquisition-style. He chose to recant publicly, but recanting was pure torture for the brilliant Galileo. Some three and a half *centuries* later, Pope John Paul II, via the Pontifical Academy of Sciences, conceded a public "my bad," confirming that "Galileo was right,"[35] after all.

---

35 Interestingly, Galileo's illegitimate children were a nonissue for the church in terms of being a "good Christian." Popes, after all, had mistresses and illegitimate kids. See how our communal beliefs about what is right/good/true change?

Many an object is not seen, though it falls
within the range of our visual ray,
because it does not come within the
range of our intellectual ray,
i.e., we are not looking for it.
So, in the largest sense,
we find only the world we look for.

—Henry David Thoreau

Quite a few years after Galileo riled all those men in funny hats, Charles Robert Darwin rocked our mutually agreed-upon "reality" (at least in Western thought) by outing natural selection, the idea that traits that make a species more robust will spread through that species, ultimately changing the whole gang.[36] It's an improve-or-perish thing. Because this theory didn't mesh well with the Western world-in-a-week view of creation—implying an ancestry that hinted at apes over Adam—it was not well accepted when it was published more than 150 years ago.

Remnants of Darwin's controversy are strong enough today—at least in my own neighborhood—that when my eldest son chose Charles Darwin as "The Man" for his fourth-grade "wax museum" project, I was asked if I wasn't "concerned that we would offend people." (Ummmm, no, until that moment I hadn't considered it a slight possibility!)

And then came those kooky quantum physicists—Jeans, Bohr, Einstein, et al. They were a small scattering of unconventional thinkers

---

36 He wasn't the only one to profess these ideas, but history has surely given him the most credit!

who realized that Newton hadn't managed to explain things very well at the level of teeny-tiny, so they took it upon themselves to figure out why. Quite a hubbub ensued, and even now, hubbubbing remains. The problem is that what we can reproduce scientifically on the subatomic level does *not* make sense to our eyes and our impenetrably prevalent common belief system.

Much of the quantum brouhaha has been the "measurement problem"— the challenge of if/how the wave function collapses. But, as has been demonstrated repeatedly in many venues, including the previously mentioned Double Slit Experiment, measuring something—adding observation or some level of consciousness—changes the outcome![37] *At the basic level of everything, consciousness is required to funnel the infinite possibilities into a "solid" something.* (Einstein, quantum's most famous door opener, could never accept the full implications of it all. As he said, famously, "I like to think that the moon is still there, even if I am not looking at it.") Physicists are, as you read this, still trying to figure out the details. But more and more scientific experts are coming to agree that consciousness just may be the wild card[38] they've never been able to completely mathematize or measure.[39]

I bring up these historical, "scientific" misfacts to point out that *for no other reason than because so many believed them, certain "facts" were "true" for hundreds of years.* Poor Copernicus. *On the Revolutions of the Heavenly Bodies* was banned in 1616, but it was not officially removed from the Don't You Dare Read It

---

37 Check out the Quantum Zeno Paradox for more "consciousness changes the experiment" insights.

38 I don't think of consciousness as "wild" at all. It's the cohesion that, once we plug into it, offers great understanding!

39 William Tiller, PhD, professor emeritus of Materials Science at Stanford and a Really Big Thinker, says this in his book *Conscious Acts of Creation*: "Under at least some conditions, human intention acts like a typical potential capable of creating robust effects in what we call physical reality." Some say he's foolish. Some say he'll go down with Copernicus. I tend to agree with the latter.

List until 1835! The pervasive perspectives were "true" enough to condone torture or at least public condemnation toward folks who weren't inclined in the "correct" direction. (A friend assures me that a couple hundred years ago, I already would have been burned at the stake for my own nonconformist ideas.) Years of "scientific proof" to the contrary mattered little. Biologist Rupert Sheldrake explains it like this: "Beliefs are powerful, not because most scientists think about them critically but because they don't."

That's exactly where we stand today in terms of accepting "reality" as consciousness versus matter. Simply because most of us still—despite all of Rutherford's early efforts—believe that only what we can see is real, and we couldn't possibly affect "reality" with our consciousness, we scoff at those scientists or regular Joes and Josies whose reality is different.

Well, not all scientists and regular Joes/Josies. Physicists are largely leading us down the rethink-what-you-thought path. And you know by now that I am not above the flagrant use of physics (or rice or poetry) to fortify my point. While I don't believe squinting through quantum peepholes into Bigness is *proof* of Bigness, it is possible to expand our viewpoint by learning new ideas. For example, even recognizing a nanospeck of quantum physics may, at the very least, open our eyes to the limitations of those eyes and what they "see." Or, more important, how we might choose to change what we see.

⌐

When you are not looking, there are waves of possibility, and when you are looking, there are positions of conscious experience.

—Dr. Amit Goswami

⌐

The thing is, right now on this planet, most of us are pretty much physicalists (not to be confused with physicists!) and believe that only what can be seen and touched is "real." Never mind that we know about Rutherford's century-old epiphany and that many of us have had intuitive moments that are physically unexplainable. Still, our common agreement about what is "solid" and "true" usually usurps the possibility of a Bigger Reality.

It is valuable to keep in mind, then, that unawareness of something does not inoculate us from its effects. For instance, it wasn't until the 1900s that Werner Heisenberg articulated the Observer Effect, a phenomenon that has influenced us all, regardless of whether we "got it" then, or "get it" now. Kind of like the concept of gravity. Even if we can't explain it,[40] or don't understand why people in a different hemisphere don't fall off the earth because they are "upside down," what we call gravity is still a force believed to keep footballs from spinning into oblivion and why (joining forces with my redheaded son) we have so many broken dishes in our home.

As a reminder, what Heisenberg said is basically this: you can't watch an electron without also affecting it. So what does it mean about observing our own electrons? For one thing, it means we would be smart to observe our observations! If (and as my beautiful soul sister, Catherine says, "*What if?*") our thoughts sway energy/matter, it is extremely important to purposefully sway our perception of what we see in the direction that will best serve us.[41]

I say "perception of what we see" because it is well documented that we filter out most of the visible data streaming our way. This is, in part, for our own well-being: we couldn't very well "see" *everything* that is

---

40 By the way, explaining gravity at the quantum level is controversial, too, so maybe most of us don't even "get" what we all call gravity!

41 By "us," I do not mean the individuals we call "us." I mean the collective, connected "us." This, of course, takes us right back to Love.

physically seeable and still function in the world. Our eyes and brains must necessarily reduce the huge amounts of input received into usable, valuable parcels for our survival. Professor Edward Tufte, according to the *New York Times*, "The Leonardo da Vinci of data," informs us that "the human retina transmits data to the brain at a rate of 10 million bits per second." You don't have to be an expert in data visualization to realize that's a honkingly ginormous amount of information. No wonder it requires paring down.

**The universe as we know it
is a joint product of the observer
and the observed.**

—Pierre Teilhard de Chardin

It's not just about *what* you see, but *how* you see it. You probably recognized some aspect of your own variable screening system ages ago. For instance, you and your best friend may have attended the same biology class and walked away with completely different experiences. Maybe you thought the professor was the "best ever," and your friend may have perceived her as the "worst in the history of the universe." Of course, the scenario also could just as well have taken place encountering a guy in a bar. But why is either case possible, if you and your very best friend (probably not *so* terribly different from each other) were both in the exact same place, at the exact same time, "experiencing" the exact same thing?

The answer seems absurdly obvious when asked this way, right? Your preferences, trained by your history and expectations, were different, creating variant filters and causing you to interpret the same data with not at all the same outcome. That's how we all roll. Our brains are constantly refining and defining for us. **We each see today based on what and how we saw yesterday.** Let's assume that system probably doesn't just happen with biology profs or potential dates in bars.

I was reminded of this a few summers back while reading the very witty and insightful Martha Beck book *Finding Your Way in a Wild New World*.[42] In one chapter, she asks her readers to list bad things that have happened in their lives (as a way to learn and possibly help others out of similarly bad experiences). I was stymied, unable to come up with a single entry to fill in the lines she so kindly left blank. "Really," I thought, "I've never had any very-bad thing happen to me." Then I turned the page and saw suggestions of terrible things we might have mentioned—here are just a few: addiction in the family (check), divorce (my parents divorced when I went to college, though really, it's hard to imagine a friendlier divorced couple), loss of a pregnancy (I've been pregnant more times than I'd like to think about and have two glorious children), getting mugged at gunpoint (does a silver switchblade just off of Central Park count?). I laughed out loud at myself (this happens a lot), but now I was *really* dumbfounded. If I'd taken a lie-detector test over my initial responses to the question, I would have passed with flying colors. My perception of "what really happened" apparently did not accommodate lugging around negative stories from my past. I honestly had viewed my life as major problem-free.

Even after taking that little poll, I still do consider myself "lucky." In fact, I think of myself as very, very lucky, a self-concept that works out tautologically in my favor, according to the experts. One creative and witty authority from the United Kingdom, Professor Richard

---

42 If you've never had the good fortune to read Martha Beck's books, please gift yourself with that pleasure! The first book I read of hers, *Expecting Adam*, showed her to be a unique thinker and a very talented writer. I've read several other books she's written and they are wonderful.

Wiseman, studies luck (among other topics) and has some quite interesting things to say about it, mostly that "lucky people generate their own good fortune."

Professor Wiseman's research is fascinating work, highlighting that *we experience what we believe to be true* (though he does not phrase it exactly like that). If we believe that we are lucky, essentially, we will be. As support for that concept, in one study, he placed newspaper ads requesting that self-described "lucky" and "unlucky" individuals contact him. Both the luckies and unluckies were given the same edition of a newspaper and were asked to count how many photos they could detect within its pages. What neither group knew ahead of time was that the clever Dr. Wiseman had stuck a game-changer close to the beginning of the exercise. In quite large print (letters about two inches tall), and taking up about half of the newspaper page, he had placed this notice: "Tell the experimenter you have seen this and win £250." Interestingly, the lucky people, those who had already expected good fortune to come their way, took only a few seconds to "count" the pictures, because on page 2, they saw the notice. The self-proclaimed "unlucky" people largely passed the winnings up, so focused were they on the counting task. Wiseman believes that lucky people "consistently encounter such [seemingly chance] opportunities, whereas unlucky people do not."

So we distill and sift. Or rather, *because many of our perceptions occur on an unconscious level, we are distilled and sifted by our prior beliefs.* Whether it is our heritage, our sad story, our hair color, our second-grade teacher, or the next-door neighbor's rooster, we relegate future possibilities and delights to concepts we schlep around with us from our own ancient history. If we think we enjoyed a "good" past, that might work out relatively well. If our personal history is nothing we'd ever want to repeat, then we're in big trouble because our tranced-out "sifter" is constrained by the stuff we know, encouraging our history to repeat itself. In either case, we cut off all sorts of wondrous possibilities—and, yes, miracles.

What we do to ourselves, then, is unconsciously create what insightful change-maker Eli Pariser calls a "Filter Bubble." In his thought-provoking book *The Filter Bubble: How the New Personalized Web Is Changing What We Read and How We Think*, Pariser explains how successive Internet searches are linked by, and respond to, our prior choices. As he elegantly writes, "Left to their own devices, personalization filters serve up a kind of invisible autopropaganda, indoctrinating us with our own ideas, amplifying our desire for things that are familiar..." He goes on to say this:

By definition, a world constructed from the familiar is a world in which there's nothing to learn. If personalization is too acute, it could prevent us from coming into contact with the mind-blowing, preconception-shattering experiences and ideas that change how we think about the world and ourselves.

Yep, that's how invisible autopropaganda works! As with Internet searches, our real-life searches are seriously constrained by the algorithms we establish from our past choices. Unless we rethink, we will forever be bound to that self-limiting course.

Most advertisers count on us *not* being able to control under-the-radar messages. In fact, successful ads depend on an effect psychologists call "priming." (When is the last time you saw miserable, unlikable people or drab colors in commercials?) Unlike memory, which involves actively grabbing an event from our mental storage room so we can look at it, priming is a phenomenon that uses our preexisting emotions/awareness about Thing One to influence a subsequent Thing Two. Priming has illustrated repeatedly, and in a broad range of topics, how quickly people can react to unconsciously influencing stimuli.[43] Psychologists have studied the effects of priming on test scores, confirming that pretest-taking information, no matter how seemingly inconspicuous, can move test scores either direction in statistically significant ways. For example, if you think of a professor—someone smart—before you answer test questions, you are likely to score better than if you conjure up "hooligans" immediately prior to question answering.

Yale's John Bargh, pretty much the forefather of priming research, studies what he calls "nonconscious or automatic influences on psychological and behavioral processes." To this end, he conducted what is probably the most famous priming test so far. He asked one group of subjects to reorder words to create sentences. They were told to select from certain "old-age-related" words like "bingo," "Florida," "wrinkles," "alone," and "bitter." Other participants had "neutral" words to organize. Sounds simple enough, but the subjects didn't know that the real test measured how quickly they entered and exited a room. Professor Bargh's researchers timed the participants' walking speed before reading words associated with old age and after reading them. The participants who worked with the "elderly" words actually walked more slowly than the neutral-word group. (In another study, participants exposed to words we associate with old age exhibited reduced memory skills!) The words on a page that were put before the participants influenced their physical behavior without them even realizing it.

In another interesting experiment, Professor Bargh primed volunteers with words we associate with impoliteness and politeness. Not surprisingly, those primed with "rude" words ended up far more likely to be conversation

---

43 Though many well-qualified researchers have "proven" priming's influence, there are other experts who strongly deny the possibilities of priming. Ironically, this takes us back to the Observer Effect, where our conscious observations/expectations collapse the field of possibilities, so that different observers, using identical criteria, find precisely what they were looking for! They fully intended to disprove priming, so their experiments yielded results aligned to their previous beliefs.

interrupters than those who had just encountered polite words. Those primed by politeness exhibited politeness right away.

In life, we are constantly in prime mode, and mostly, we don't even know it. It is why **we must consciously create for our brains the inputs we prefer, or be subjected to the inputs others prefer.** It is also why, as parents, or bosses, or teachers, or friends, we should note how, even without a PhD, or any sort of statistical analysis, we subject those around us to our own priming. If you say to your daughter, "You know how you always go downhill during finals. You really have trouble focusing, and you blow your course averages because of your final exams," it is likely she will treat that information exactly how psychology subjects responded to "wrinkles" and "alone." We always message what our history tells us we should "see," even if it's not what we really want to create as our vision!

That we see what is not necessarily there, and vice versa, should not really surprise us: optical illusions have told us that for years. I remember discovering optical illusions ages ago during elementary school and being very surprised. Did I see things correctly, or not? Sure, our eyes collect the light reflecting off images, but our brains tell us what we are "seeing." As with what we "see" happening all around us, this can lead us to incorrect conclusions.

Maybe you remember this well-known drawing of the old woman/young woman from a late-1800s German postcard. In the picture, do you see the side/back of a young woman's head, or do see a profile of an old woman? (Hint: the younger woman's necklace is the older woman's mouth.) For most people, when we tell our brain to see the old woman, she usually "pops out." When we instruct our brain to see the young woman, she generally appears before our eyes, too. How does that happen so immediately? Because, *at some level, we will always see what we tell ourselves to see*...and this happens whether or not we are aware the process is going on (and we are most frequently in the "or not" department!).

There is an example on my website that helps bring this idea home. Basically, color words (red, blue, green, and so on) are written in colors *other* than the color they represent. That is, we see the letters O-R-A-N-G-E written in purple ink: a total head fake! For most of us, our brain wants us to "read" the *color*, not the actual word. Our brains will always fill in the gaps with stuff we've trained them to expect. (This is much better understood in color, so please head to KellyCorbet.com and search for the visual. It will make more sense, I promise!)

 For a final example of visual trickery, here is a picture of the tile wall in front of the ladies' bathroom at San Francisco's Exploratorium. It consists of black and white square tiles, right? Yes, but how those same-shaped, right-angled tiles are aligned leads our eyes to perceive something wavy, or concave. We can easily establish that what we "see" isn't the truth of what is happening right before us, and yet...

If all these incomplete interpretations aren't enough, there is also the matter of what Arien Mack and Irvin Rock named "inattentional blindness." This is the (often-surprising) failure to notice what should be completely "seeable" because of our inattention—or maybe our attention directed to something else. Again, this illustrates that *we find what we look for; we literally become blind to something merely because our focus is elsewhere*. You may have seen the well-known video demonstrating the Invisible Gorilla experiment.[44] Daniel Simons and Christopher Chabris created an exercise that dramatically highlights how we can miss something—even when it's big *and* furry *and* looking directly at us—if we have told ourselves to seek something different. I hate to spoil the punch line of this Ig Nobel Prize in Psychology-winning work, but basically, when people are asked to count basketball passes among teammates, *about half of them completely miss a large "gorilla" strolling through the middle of the action!*[45] After you've watched the clip (assuming you had no advance hints), when you're asked if you saw a gorilla, you may not be able to imagine what the ridiculous researchers are thinking. When you watch again, keeping your eyes open for a gorilla, well, you can't imagine what *you* were thinking! (It is a fun video to share. My kids loved it.)

The world appears to you so overwhelmingly real because you think of it all the time.
Cease thinking of it and it will dissolve into the mist.

—Nisargadatta Maharaj

Mostly we find such "tricks" interesting and fun, and we tend to stop there, not extrapolating the idea that illusions might be taken for "real" in situations other than silly little optical stunts. *Like our lives.* What if our Real Joy is gorillaesque in its right-thereness, and we have just trained our eyes on passing basketballs? Why would it make sense that phenomena

---

44 If you haven't, look it up right now, because it's great. You can find it here: http://www.theinvisiblegorilla.com/gorilla_experiment.html.

45 When Professor Wiseman shows this video, he "primes" the audience with a little competition—like having women compete against men—and can reduce the percentage of people who can see the gorilla to as low as 5 percent!

such as inattentional blindness and priming would happen only to volunteers taking psychology tests at Harvard or Yale?

They do not.

My point of bringing up all these forms of deliberate optical/brain trickery is really just to underscore that *believing is seeing, rather than the other way around.* And that so much of what we "perceive" isn't really believable or even "true"!

The *real* trick, then, is reorienting our eyes and brains past the unconscious autofilter and directing what we want them to see, overriding our historical expectations. What kind of informational morsels do we want our eyes and brains to feed us? How do we want our brains to navigate our speed-processing retinal viewfinder? I have found that it takes just a little consciousness on our part. It isn't "hard" at all; it's just so very, very, very different from what we normally do!

Fortunately, we do not have to rely on random or anticipated good luck or on special training in illusions to help us expand our conscious choices. Improved consciousness comes from practice. The more you practice...

The following exercise is a simple, fun way to practice reteaching our sifters.

EXERCISE 5: Thank-Off

GO FOR IT!

One of my sons dances hip-hop, so we have attended Stand Your Ground dance-offs. They are energetic, Love-filled, and incredibly fun events to watch. They work like this: two dancers perform their best moves "against" each other, in a friendly, in-your-face way. If one dancer pulls out a great move (or two or three), the other dancer tries to reach even higher. The judges vote on a winner immediately, until the winners have all danced their way to the finals to determine *the* winner. The truth is, we *all* win, thanks to so much joy being generated in the room!

The Thank-Off game is sort of like that, but without the dancing (well, I'd never tell anyone *not* to dance, so go ahead, if you feel the urge!). We sometimes play it on the way to school, each trying to come up with better and better thankfulness moves. It's a magical way to shift any less-than-positive energy, and I love knowing my kids have started their daily education by actively "dancing" with the good stuff.

1. One person starts by saying something he is thankful for that day. It can be generic ("kind friends") or specific ("the colorful birthday card our darling first-grade neighbor made me"). They can build on each other, such as "I am thankful for quesadillas" and "I am thankful quesadillas are so easy to make!" They can be totally random. One morning, my oldest son reported that he is thankful for Nicolas Cage. Huh? That started a funny discussion of the movies he has seen, what he thinks makes a good actor, and similar topics. (I was very thankful for the discussion!)
2. We each take turns naming something that brings up a feeling of gratefulness in our hearts. It's important to let everyone say anything, rather than "guiding" him/her not to be silly or off-track. There is no "right" or "wrong." Anyway, sometimes "off-track" can be the biggest thing of all to be grateful for!
3. Enjoy your grateful day that is sure to be filled with lots of inspiring things that you've primed yourself for!

And above all,
watch with glittering eyes
the whole world around you because
the greatest secrets are always hidden
in the most unlikely places.

—Roald Dahl

Counting blessings (instead of miseries) predisposes us to "luck" and miracles that our old focus might have obscured. The poet Muriel Rukeyser tells us, "The universe is made of stories, not of atoms." We can continue being reactive to the stories all around us, *or* we can always choose to be proactive and control the input to the stories we tell and live. As I will continue to say, that necessitates that we wake up a bit (repent!) because most of us are on didn't-even-know-it autopilot. We've been "asleep" for so long that even when we *think* we are aware of something while it's happening, we may remain unaware of its impact on us.

For example, one morning I was uncharacteristically early for a Pilates class, so I stepped on the treadmill just outside the Pilates room. It was a few days after the devastating school shooting in Newtown, Connecticut, and though my focus was not helpful in the slightest, I admit that I had been unable to stop crying about it. I was somehow hoping for good news then, when I saw an expert already on the screen in front of me discussing the latest details. I'd been treading for only a couple minutes—going slowly, so as not to actually sweat—when the machine started blinking wildly at me, demanding that I *stop*! My heart rate (*Blink! Blink!*) was exceeding (*Blink! Blink! Blink!*) safe limits! I had never caused such a response in a machine before. What the heck was going on? Then it occurred to me:

my heartbeat—certainly not the fleetness of my feet—went out of control gauging my emotional response to the news!

Now, I like to fancy myself a relatively in-tune kind of gal. I don't tend to overreact. I meditate lots and can mostly keep myself in calmness. Not always, but mostly. Yet my body was freaking out! Somehow, *completely without my conscious knowledge*, some unrevealed part of me sent high doses of cortisol—and who knows what else—speedballing through my cells, amping up my heart to a level that greatly concerned the protective treadmill!

The treadmill incident cannot have been the only time my cells responded to outside stimuli without mentioning it to the "conscious" part of me. It was just the first time I was attached to an external feedback device kind enough to clue me in. I'm sharing this because I suspect I'm not alone and because for each of us, much sifting and intake occurs below our perceived radar (again, based on what we have sucked in and carted with us from the past, or where we set our focus).

My treadmill experience really shocked me and, in so doing, helped me realize how much more is obscured under my own hood than I'd ever assumed. Additionally, and much to my surprise, it helped me perceive ill health in a way that finally made more sense to me. In the past, I could never satisfactorily reconcile my belief that our choices create our own "reality" with regard to human suffering and illness. Like anyone wakes up one day and thinks, "Wow, wouldn't it be great if I got cancer next week." Ridiculous! But if commercials, teachers, psychology tests, history books, religions, parents, rap songs, boyfriends, *interviewees on TV*, and every other source of "information" endlessly "instruct" us—prime us—those unwitting tugs on our psyche contort our subliminal intentions in ways we cannot predict. Or sometimes even discern. Gary Zukav, in his important classic *Seat of the Soul*, puts it succinctly: "If you have conflicting intentions, you will be torn because both dynamics will be set in motion and oppose each other." He warns us that by not being aware of our subliminal will, the intention with more muscle will win.

In the case of the Newtown shooting, my unintended intention to personalize the drama won out over any intention to send Love. Not only did it affect my body negatively (for one thing, stress is a *very* anti-immune activity!), but it did not bring Love to a place of pain. I created no room for a miracle to show up because of my own unconsciousness. After I realized that, I began sending Love (in place of worry) to the people of Newtown. When I meditate now, I try to set my mindful intentions for sending Love only, rather than focussing on the misery of the "problem." No negativity or less-than-helpful energy!

⌣⟶

We don't see things as they are;
we see them as we are.

—*The Talmud*

⌣⟶

A Course in Miracles tells us, "You see what you expect, and you *expect* what you *invite*."[46] If we don't like what we see in our lives, we really can make the choice to tell a different story to ourselves and our world, one more likely to invite in greater happiness. (Just because this is nothing we've ever done in the past does not mean we can't bring on the joy now!) In essence, making pain the story we tell share with the world—and maybe even more important, share with our atomic foundation—will make sure that what we "see" in our lives will reflect just that.[47]

---

46 *A Course in Miracles*, T-22.VII.5:1.

47 To be very clear: I do not believe that babies who get cancer, or victims of incomprehensible shootings, war, or abuse, for example, are "at fault" or "to blame" in any way whatsoever! *Not at all!* My theory on that one has to do with our soul's "individual" purpose and is beyond my intentions for this little book.

This may not mean that the scene changes all that much, but our *perception* of the play being acted out can change absolutely everything.

EXERCISE 6: Prime Yourself

GO FOR IT!

We have already practiced "priming" exercises in this book, but this time we will have in our awareness the studies on priming and inattentional blindness (which, ironically, will prime us and hopefully forestall any inattentional blindness!).

1. Look around your home as if you were in it for the first time. What do you see? Are there pictures of loved ones? Flowers? Kindergarten art projects from the little girl across the street taped to the walls (sure to make anyone smile)? In short, is there stuff you like that creates a prime-you-toward-more-joy ambiance? Or do you have mountains of unpaid bills and projects left half-done and piled high, reminding you constantly that you are disorganized/a bad person/in debt?
2. Consciously remove what makes you feel bad. Put it away where it doesn't get to prime you on a regular basis. I'm not saying ignore your bills; I'm just saying it's a better idea to have them put neatly in some drawer (and pay them as soon as you can) than to have them taunt you hourly by teetering on the kitchen counter. Now replace some of the bothersome items with things that make you happy (and happiness might be pure, unobstructed space!).
3. By making your surroundings more joy-invoking, you will incline yourself toward more joy without even having to think about it!

The world is, thankfully, filled with sparkling and uplifting examples of people who have created happiness for themselves from little more than their mindful choices. Susan Spencer-Wendel was a woman, who by any "logical" metric, could have declared for herself (and the world) a very tragic tale. Instead she consciously selected joy. We are very fortunate she chronicled that decision. She illustrated that *how we deal with what we've been dealt will determine the quality of our life.*

In her beautiful memoir *Until I Say Good-Bye: My Year of Living with Joy,* Susan wrote heroically and humorously about her joy choice. Smack-dab in the middle of a great life, blessed with three children, a loving husband, and a successful career, she was diagnosed with ALS, amyotrophic lateral sclerosis, known more commonly as Lou Gehrig's disease. ALS is a neurodegenerative disease for which there is currently no cure or even treatment, so those afflicted must watch their bodies devitalize into paralysis, while their brains remain sidelined witnesses. Making mighty use of her talented brain, however, and the one thumb that still acceded to her will, Susan painstakingly plunked out her inspirational memoir *on her phone!*

A full life cut short by a body-ravaging disease feels undeniably sad, no matter how well she wrote about the circumstance, but this talented, insightful woman never aimed for pity, only joy. Referencing her diminishing physical capabilities, she acknowledged that she had a "choice" over her feelings. She chose to see the good stuff.

For me, a secondary message underlying Susan's incredibly moving story has to do with releasing attachments to what we think joy "should" look like as defined by our anachronistic filter bubble, the world, or any other source besides our true source. She decided *not* to define joy via her body, which—with or without physical illness—is a brilliant tactic.

You have probably already noted that our culture is *obsessed* with bodies. Whether decorating them, feeding them, making them better, skinnying or fattening them, adding or subtracting parts to and from them, we spend lots and lots of time, money, and energy focusing on our bodies! We even allow what seems to be going on with our bodies to dominate how we feel. People joke about "bad hair days" and "shoe therapy," but the humor reveals an undeniable truth—that much of our happiness seems oh-so-physical-body-dependent.

Our bodies are not the dispatchers of joy or disappointment we perceive them to be (regardless of the nitrogazillion dollars spent on advertising to the contrary). If great hair days or walking around in clothing of a certain label could architect joy, we would probably have more happy people on this planet. But, despite what things mostly *look like*, the happiness equation has absolutely nothing to do with our bodies. Susan powerfully illustrated that.

Our flesh and bones are just the impermanent part of us. They serve as "space suits" in which to play, learn, Love, and grow. But bodies, as we all know, are transitory and confirm that fact every single day. They do look solid, more or less, so we think they are incontrovertible, but in fact, the "you" now is not the "you" of even a few weeks ago. The vast majority of our cells come and go. Our skin cells get replaced about every two weeks, and even our skeletons get a cellular makeover about every ten years or so. And despite national statistics that seem to point to the contrary, approximately 10 percent of our fat cells even turn over each year. So why depend on these ever-changing physical costumes we don for our happiness, when changeless Love is gently waiting for us to notice it?

That said, as long as we are walking around in bodies, we might as well make the best use of them we can. *Rather than letting our bodies dictate our emotions, we should consciously direct how our bodies feel.* Surely the multitude of messages we receive consciously and unconsciously impacts our bodies. Maybe various body-image messaging offers just a little directional push here and there, but repeatedly, those pushes can change our biology. If every day in the news we read that "cold and flu season is here," or that scientists have now discovered that "using XYZ is bad for us," or some food is "the worst thing we can eat," what does our belief-system matrix do with that information?

 

**There are realities existing apart
from our sense perceptions.**

— Max Planck

 

I had my own little cookie-reality experience that I'm absolutely certain influenced my perspective of how much this body I'm wearing should weigh. After church one Sunday ages ago, while standing near the goodies table, an older gentleman I'd never met pointed to the sweet array and announced to me, "I can eat any of this I want. I decided a long time ago that calories were never going to cause weight issues." He then proceeded to pile cookies precariously on his plate, smiling very satisfactorily. I hadn't thought much about calories before that minute (this was before anorexia and bulimia had made their entrance into common Western awareness), but I did think his idea sounded like a good one. He looked healthy and happy, so—I know this might sound odd—right then and there, I accepted that the same could work for me. And then I "felt" it click in. I just accepted that such an idea could be my truth. That was about a thousand and three years ago, and so far, so good!

And as long as I'm on the topic of belief influencing our physicality, what about aging? Why do we age? Because we believe we must? Are wrinkles and arthritis inevitable? Why? Years ago, I read that one of my physics crushes, the Nobel-winning, bongo-playing Richard Feynman, asserted that there's nothing biologically certain about having to age. Or that's what I *thought* he said, so I proceeded through the years with that information in my attitude and in my cells. (I mean, if a Nobel Prize winner said so…) It turns out that what he actually said was "There is nothing in biology yet found that indicates the inevitability of death." OK, so I was just interpolating. But why not? I mean, roses don't look worse at a certain age, do they? Why should we? My oak trees look more glorious each and every year. Why not follow that cue? What if we imagined "old age" with completely different adjectives? What if, before subliminally applying Professor Bargh's "wrinkles in Florida" experiment to our own lives, we primed ourselves differently about aging?

What if?

⌐⟋

"I'm just one hundred and one, five months, and a day."

"I can't believe that!" said Alice.

"Can't you?" the Queen said in a pitying tone. "Try again: draw a long breath and shut your eyes."

Alice laughed. "There's no use trying," she said. "One can't believe impossible things."

"I dare say you haven't had much practice," said the Queen. "When I was your age, I always did it for half an hour a day. Why, sometimes I've believed as many as six impossible things before breakfast."[48]

⌐⟋

---

48 You probably already know this is from Lewis Carroll's *Through the Looking-Glass, and What Alice Found There.*

So, yes, I'm saying that what we believe can age us...or help us see primates dodging basketballs...or create a healthy body, where once there was a "sick" one...or become educated, even if nobody in our family has ever done so...or help create a world that remembers Love. The list of new possibilities is endless! Because, after all, **what we think, we see.**

What do *you* want to see?

An excellent demonstration of how "priming" can affect our physical age was conducted by Harvard's deep-thinking and very creative Dr. Ellen J. Langer in 1979. It was called the "Counterclockwise Study," in which she and her students "duplicated" 1959. She recruited two groups of men in their late seventies or early eighties to relive a week of that year. For both groups, everything at the retro experiment site was perfectly 1959: the environment was decorated as though 1960 had not yet arrived. Magazines and movies—*Ben Hur* and *Some Like It Hot*—reinforced the era. TV shows could have included *The Ed Sullivan Show*, *Perry Mason*, and *Bonanza*.

But here's how the two groups differed: the men in the first group were instructed to act as if they were really, truly living in 1959. They displayed pictures of themselves from that year and wrote autobiographical information as if 1959 were the current year. They were required to converse using only information that would have been available in that year. "Current" topics might have included Castro's new position as prime minister of Cuba. They engaged in a "postgame" emotional discussion about the Giants losing to the Baltimore Colts in the NFL championship. They listened to the likes of Rosemary Clooney and Perry Como, as if they were actually tuning into a radio station. The whole 1959 experience was in the "present tense."

A week later, the second group of volunteers (the control group) visited the same site and surrounded themselves similarly, but with one major difference: the year 1959 was a memory—history. Biographical information was written with a past-tense frame of reference. Pictures of the participants were from 1979, not 1959. They could talk about the past that was propped up all around them, but in nostalgic terms. So although the physical ambiance was the same, the mental ambiance for each group was completely different.

Both groups registered improved hearing and memory, increased weight, and a better grip after a week in 1959. The group that actually "lived" the year 1959, however, looked younger than the control group, according to "objective observers" who examined pictures taken at the end of the retro week. Even though they had not been told the details of the experiment, the observers deemed that the men who lived "as if" all looked younger than the "remember when" control group. Not only that, "youngerness" was measurable: the "real" 1959ers did better on intelligence tests and demonstrated decreased arthritis symptoms (better flexibility in their joints, and their fingers measured longer because they could straighten them out!).

In her compelling book *Counterclockwise*, Langer writes, "It is not primarily our physical selves that limit us but rather our minds about our physical limits. Now I accept none of the medical wisdom regarding the courses our diseases must take as necessarily true."[49]

⟨⟩

**Every thought you have makes up some segment of the world you see.
It is with your thoughts, then,
that we must work if your perception of the world is to be changed.**

—*A Course in Miracles*,
W-pI.23.2:4-5

⟨⟩

---

49 *Counterclockwise*, Langer, p. 11.

So, then, back to aging…why do we age? Is it because we think we must? What would happen if we all rethought the "inevitability" of getting old? If men in their seventies and eighties can grow younger in a week by what they feed their brains, what about the rest of us?

If nothing else, *examples of other people doing something "impossible" allow our brains to create attainableness: they help us rethink what we choose to see*. And this doesn't happen just when it comes to growing older or younger. Cases of people jumping the belief fence and opening up all-new acreage for human endeavors are surprisingly plentiful. One of the most famous is the four-minute-mile barrier. It is one of my favorite examples of how to rupture an obstinate, limiting collective belief about our physical possibilities. Back in 1954, Englishman Roger Bannister was the first to break that long-sought-after mile record at 3:59 minutes. And, with the updated belief system of the "possible" pierced, just a few weeks later, an Australian bettered the record! Pop! (The current record has subsequently been shaved by more than 15 seconds.)

We can go as fast and as far as we *think* we can!

$\backsim$

We should split the sack of this
culture and stick our heads out.

—Rumi

$\backsim$

CHAPTER 5
The Illusion of Time

Time has no independent existence apart from
the order of events by which we measure it.

—ALBERT EINSTEIN

Consider heaven
as a world-weary stranger
asleep in your heart.

—ABERJHANI

MY HUSBAND ASSURES ME IT'S not so easy to live with someone who doesn't believe in time. This observation is frequently lobbed as I dash out to the garage (shoes in one hand, purse in the other, cell phone under my chin) and leap in the car he's been waiting in. He's kidding, of course. I'm pretty sure.

When I say I don't believe in time, I don't mean that I can't make it to a meeting when everyone else does (theoretically) or wish a friend "Happy Birthday!" on the right day. What I mean is this: *what we call time is a made-up, linear construct that limits us in ways we don't even realize* because most of us have probably never considered its truthiness.

Well, that's not exactly accurate. We have probably all marveled at time's inconsistency during our lives. Who hasn't been rapt in conversation, only to be stunned by glancing at the hour? On my first date with my husband, for example, time did a crazy, warped-out trick that shocked us both.

We were dining at a week-new San Francisco restaurant, one that hadn't quite worked out all the kinks. First, we ordered wines from the menu that weren't actually available yet (so we let the waiter choose for us). Next, food started making its way to our table before we even ordered. Finally, the maître d' appeared tableside and huffed, "Sir! Is your car parked with the valet? We've been closed for an hour and a half!" My initial thought was "Wow, this place is never going to make it, closing so early!" And then I looked around. Only one tired car parker and a single disgusted maître d' remained with us in the previously packed dining room. You could have knocked me over with a feather! How did all those loud people get up to leave without my noticing? And even more surprising, how on earth could five and a half hours have flashed by like that?

The only reason for time is so that everything doesn't happen at once.

—ALBERT EINSTEIN

Besides shrinking, time is also pretty good at stretching. Think about it—counting down the moments until your ninth birthday party, waiting for your cell phone to recharge, looking for those two pink lines to appear on your pregnancy-test stick, holding for tech support to help with your crashed computer—don't so many things take much longer than a clock can accurately register? As Einstein famously said, "When a man sits with a pretty girl for an hour, it seems like a minute. But let him sit on a hot stove for a minute, and it's longer than any hour." Our experiences are all so relative to our perspective!

You might be thinking, "That's ridiculous, Kelly. It just *seems* like time changes according to our situation." OK, but isn't it our "perception" that invented the images we saw/didn't see/experienced in the previous chapters (and every part of our lives)? Our perception *is* what creates our "reality." Time exists as we perceive it.[50]

With that said, let me remind you about the two major gripes I have with our entrenched belief in time. The first is that most of our "knowledge" is based on the "past," which is extremely limiting (recall all the sifting our brain does to allow only a tiny bit of information to squeeze in). Second, we seem to think we'll need tons of time if we ever hope to achieve any level of enlightenment. But...what if we decided that our tomorrow didn't absolutely need to be based on our yesterday and that reaching a higher level of spiritual connectedness could happen just by our allowing it?

What if?

Seriously, don't we base our future possibilities on our perception of likely outcomes that are dictated from our past? We are framed within, obligated to, and often damaged by events that occurred *years* ago. Our staunch adherence to our history looms over all our potential futures, and

---

50 What we segment out as a "yesterday-today-tomorrow" phenomenon (time) is actually a Big Honkin' Now, or everywhen. And because that is such a big honkin' concept, I'm thankful that understanding it is not requisite to living a happier, blissed-out life. Phew! No need to completely alter your view of time in this little chapter. Should you care to go deeper, however, myriad scientific brainiacs *and* spiritual way-finders have covered the topic using geometry, astrophysics, poetry, and theories that I could only regurgitate ineptly. Here I'm merely inviting you to think differently about time as a way of helping you open to "biggerness."

chops off untold possibilities, because they are, literally, *unimaginable*. We all know people (I have been one of them) who carry the past around, making it their obligatory story:

* I can't go to New York! When I was five, I got lost in a big parade, and I'm still petrified of big crowds.
* My mother was an alcoholic, so now (even though I'm sixty-seven) I don't think I can count on anyone.
* My father left my mother and my husband left *me*. See?
* My family has always been poor. We will never know what it's like to be debt-free.

What if our adhesion to past expectations is the *reason* we got cheated on, never earned much money, found risk too risky—expecting it all as we did? What if, by interpreting ourselves as unworthy at some level, we sought out situations to prove our past-based beliefs about ourselves to be true? Please understand that I am *not* saying we invite this stuff consciously. That's exactly my point! We are *unconscious* to so much. I'm hoping that by "repenting," we can call back our consciousness, and by being conscious, recreate a more Love-filled scenario!

EXERCISE 7: Badnesia

GO FOR IT!

When you wake up tomorrow, pretend you have a big case of "badnesia"—that for just one day, you can't remember a ding-dang *bad* thing that happened in your life history (or on the planet, for that matter). We've all seen movies or soap operas in which amnesia creates a whole new reality for the person experiencing it, as well as for every character around him because he's just not acting like his "old self." This is your chance to star in your own miniseries about selective amnesia, without the downside of a head injury or doctor bills. I'm *not* saying don't go to work, or ditch your responsibilities, or disregard someone who needs help. I'm merely suggesting that for one day, you wipe your slate clean of a negative past. For twenty-four hours, stop reviewing the history book you call your life, and tell a new story…one with lighter baggage!

Here are some suggestions:

1. Start your morning with a decision—a proclamation to yourself—to withdraw only positive "investments" (or memories) from your memory bank. There's nothing valuable (or even slightly interesting, frankly) in complaining to everyone how your insomnia kept you awake since 2:00 a.m. And I promise, "witty" and "delightful" are not words that spring to the minds of those who have listened to that detailed description of your horrible, rotten, no good, very bad divorce for the thirty-seventh time. Moreover, none of this rehashing is helpful to *you*. Don't get me wrong: I'm not saying we should live our lives in deference to other people's topics of interest. Nor am I saying we should squish down feelings that feel real and are swirling in our bodies. I'm simply suggesting that we avoid actively nurturing the negative feelings. I'm proposing that there's no helpful reason to review ad nauseam all those bad-the-first-time-why-repeat-them? events in life. It just doesn't serve us.

2. Listen to yourself throughout the day. Become an "objective observer" in your own conversations. Do you complain about your mother-in-law over coffee with your coworker? Do you expect your child to forget his homework like he has done 493 times before, all the while imagining the extra work you'll have to do if he forgets it yet again? Do you find yourself preparing for "battles" that may never come

about? ("Well, if he says *this*, then I'll just say *that*, and...")
Such examples are all based on what you've experienced in
the past, so gently brush them off, like lint, and go forward
without allowing them—or *inviting* them—to cling to you.

3. If someone starts to complain that Mary Ann in accounting
is driving her nuts—"Can you believe she clips her nails at
her desk? And if she has one more phone fight with her boy-
friend..."—rather than join in the verbal dump, creatively
change the conversation. Consciously elect not to engage in
negative chitchat. (And while you're at it, try not to dis the
person who was just dissing Mary Ann. Instead, thank her
silently for helping you flex your "repenting muscle.")

4. By evaporating the negativity—by simply not engaging
it—we create a space for more happiness to enter. (It's really hard for happiness to find room when we are elbowing
it out with all the things that make us mad.)

5. Enjoy a fabulous badnesia day, unencumbered by the past,
and just *be* in the moment you are in! As Papaji said, "Now
is the time to have a direct introduction to this moment.
This moment is free of time, of mind, of any notions.
Introduce yourself to this moment."

If you are like most people, your badnesia day probably surprised you.
By paying attention, you likely saw some bit of habitual reference to past
negativity sneak through your day, and perhaps even whack you upside the
head. Our culture currently (though I hope not for long) seems to offer
more support for hostility or bitterness (if it's not too strong) than for happiness. Every newspaper publisher knows that bad news sells better than
"wimpy, feel-good" stuff.

But why allow the current norm to keep us from our innate worth and
joy? By regularly practicing the exercise above on "little" things, we will

radically help repent our experiences to include more positives. Actively looking for better plops us right in its tree-lined neighborhood.

**For the Present is the point at which
time touches eternity.**

—C. S. Lewis

Why Wait for Bliss?

So, about my second time-related gripe: we act as if blissyness[51] can be attained only through kicking the bucket (and even then, blissless hell seems to be an option in more than a few religious circles) or logging infinite hours on bended knees. I'm pretty much saying that "heaven" could be right here, right now, if we only invited it and expected it to arrive. As I mentioned, bliss/grace/connection to Source is already here, anyway, right in front of us. Again, I'm not making this stuff up. When a few Pharisees wondered when the kingdom of heaven would show up, Jesus replied, "Neither shall they say, 'Lo here, or lo there! For behold the kingdom of God is within you.'"[52]

What is "time," anyway? Is it a concept dependent on space as in "spacetime" and Einstein's relativity theories? Is it motion? Is it imagined? What does it mean when we see a star "now," but what we are really seeing—depending on its distance from us—is what it looked like a couple years ago, or maybe even thousands of years ago? I remember when

---

51 It can also be called grace, salvation, enlightenment—it answers to a lot of pseudonyms.
52 Luke 17:21.

I learned that the stars I could see in the sky were only "memories." How confusing is that?

So, then, can we measure something nobody can even accurately define? Maybe time is just measuring something invented, something that doesn't really matter...

Really, all the exercises in this book have been aimed at helping us realize that bliss *can* be right here, right now, in every moment, and indipendent of time. My stunningly insightful friend Jenn is beautiful, brilliant, and wise, and she makes a mean goat cheese. She is also an excellent example of how shifting our thoughts can shift our experience of what's really going on. She says everything flipped for her when she decided to change her perspective (a decision ushered in by consciously attending gratefulness, reading gratefulness.org, and other memory joggers.) Instead of complaining about having to spend so much time and money at the grocery store, she *decided* to feel grateful she could afford to buy good food for her family. And how convenient to have it all gathered together for her in one place! Chores around the house? How *lucky* she has such a Love-filled place to lay her head at night, laugh with her family, and, yes, spit 'n' polish things from time to time! She tells me she just decided, and everything "changed." While I hate to quibble with my inspiring friend, I must point out the obvious here: *nothing* changed but her perspective! And it took her no "time." (She says she still has to remind herself not to grumble on occasion—like we all do—but her conscious decision has changed the whole equation.)

So, how to use your perception of time to your highest advantage? Spend it going nowhere, aka with your highest self. Sit quietly, and feel your heart space. I understand, that sounds a bit "out there," but by now in the book, I'm hoping you can feel what I mean when I say "heart space." That is your "kingdom of heaven." Waiting for you in the silence I haven't been too silent about!

We're such a gang of doers, it's hard to imagine that "*not* doing" would be a goal for any but the laziest of sorts: the kind who never succeed, who never "go" anywhere. And really, isn't the kingdom of heaven, like, a super-important place? Far away and probably on a very steep incline? Shouldn't we train for it? Get up at 5:30 a.m. to dash "there," and at least break a sweat while passing out alms along the way?

Um, no.

There's nothing you have to be, do, or get in order to find bliss. Just slow down, listen, and remember.

To help buck the prejudice that we all need to be "doing" something all the time to reach whatever goals we have (including, ironically, finding grace), I share the following list—a brief lineup of folks you may recognize, who made it their *daily* habit to spend time going inside themselves:

1. Oprah Winfrey
2. Tina Turner
3. Paul McCartney
4. Stevie Wonder
5. Gisele Bündchen
6. Howard Stern
7. Kurt Vonnegut
8. Clint Eastwood
9. Madonna
10. Al Gore

All these folks have noted how important getting quiet has been for them and how it contributed to what we generally consider their "success." I don't believe that spending time in meditation will turn us all into an Oprah or a Howard Stern, but I think that getting quiet and listening, really listening, is the key to finding our own version of "success." The more we learn to listen, the more "successful" we become.[53]

The purpose of "time" is just to remember our truth that exists beyond it!

⌐⁓

Now, what about those two times, past and future: in what sense do they have real being, if the past no longer exists and the future does not exist yet? As for present time, if that were always present and never slipped away into the past, it would not be time at all; it would be eternity. If, therefore, the present's only claim to be called "time" is that it is slipping away into the past, how can we assert that this thing *is*, when its only title to being is that it will soon cease to be? In other words, we cannot really say that time exists, except because it tends to non-being.

—SAINT AUGUSTINE[54]

⌐⁓

---

53 And you know "success" here can be completely independent of commas on a bank statement, right? It's however *you* define it, which may be in terms of master nap taker, splendiferous soup maker, and, certainly, peace rememberer.
54 This is from my favorite translation of St. Augustine's work, *The Confessions: Saint Augustine of Hippo*. It was translated by Maria Boulding, O.S.B, and edited by David Vincent Meconi, S. J. p. 344. Ignatius Press, 2012.

CHAPTER 6

Silence, Please!

⟋

God speaks in the silence of the heart.
Listening is the beginning of prayer.

—MOTHER TERESA

Wherever you are is the entry point.

—KABIR

IT IS NOT WITHOUT EMBARRASSMENT that I reveal my former high-school title of "Most Talkative." My children horrifyingly confirm that my verbosity thrives these many decades hence. I frequently find myself chatting with brand-new friends in the produce aisle, a restaurant, or the post office. In addition, my darling teenager teeth-grittingly informs that me I laugh more loudly than anyone else on the planet ever has. I am only admitting this lengthy, huge, and disconcerting dearth of natural silence to absolutely assure you that if *I* can meditate/pray/connect in stillness, believe me, *anyone* can![55] True fact.

---

55 Disclaimer: yes, I can "Zen out" much of the time, but I am *not* saying I totally live in a state of pure serenity. I'm heading that direction, though.

From here on, I'll mostly use the phrase "plug in" when referring to that magical, helpful, necessary stillness because "pray" and "meditate" escort a gazillion and two years' worth of preconceptions, opinions, and dogma to the conversation. "Praying" has been commandeered by judgment or smallness too many times, and the inner stillness I propose here bears no resemblance to that kind of thinking. I have heard people discover their much-loved neighbor to be Buddhist, and commence to pray for her, lest she go to hell (they were good Christians). We've probably all witnessed football teams bow down for scoring intercessions from the Big Guy before a game. (How does that work when *both* teams implore with equal vehemence?) Given this backdrop, and if we are "repenting" after all, I suspect that a minimal-history phrase could be helpful here. Hence, "plug in"[56]!

I like the phrase "plug in" for more than just its lack of baggage. Plugging in implies a trusted source of energy already flowing, just waiting to be accessed. Those of us who live in developed countries can usually plug in our computers, phones, vacuums, and toasters, almost never wondering if the power will be available to energize whatever needs it. It's just "there." The same is true when we "plug in" to our higher selves. *Any time we open our heart to Love, we are plugging in.*

In case you haven't noticed, you've been "plugging in" every time you've practiced one of the little exercises in this book (and you *have* been practicing those exercises, right? Who doesn't have three minutes?) If you are like most of my "research assistants," you have already experienced a shift closer to bliss.

Over the years, I've tried a gazillion and four ways to plug in. I've sat stiffly for hours, alone and in groups; walked labyrinths; chanted; sung; positioned my hands and head just so; danced; listened to experts

---

56 And when, for the sake of variety, I do toss in those old, familiar phrases like "pray" and "meditate," please treat them kindly and without prejudice.

addressing me through earbuds; stood quietly in my garden, breathing in my roses; and probably just as many other ways I've long forgotten. To me, all the variations boil down to two prongs of plugging in; they enhance each other, kind of like how peanut butter and jelly work in a sandwich. The peanut butter holds everything together. The jelly makes it easier to swallow. The "peanut butter" is what we consider traditional prayer or meditation: a time apart for silence and going within. It's the protein. It's the foundation. The second *very valuable* way to plug in is simply to consciously call peace into any moment, any place, and any time. That's the jelly. Metaphorically speaking, a jelly-only sandwich probably couldn't sustain you nutritionally, but it definitely makes the sandwich more delicious when added to the peanut butter.

⇛

This inner wisdom-center is your personal Secret Place,
the Secret Place of the Most High,
and if you want to become fully conscious of it…
you need only to be still—
very, very, very still—
and practice the long-lost art of "listening."

—Ruby Nelson

⇛

A great many experts have written books on specific ways to meditate, so I won't go into meditating minutiae here. Besides, I think *by just listening, we will all find our own style of silence.* Where I think my meditative ideas might add value—far more than suggesting how to sit, breathe, or situate your hands—is in discussing the general plugging-in purlieu.

I will explain the big picture way it works *for me*. In both PB&J cases, I intentionally "drop down" from my head to my heart space—first by focusing on the *idea* of Love, then by experiencing the *feelings* of Love. You've probably recognized this in the previous exercises. Taking the "elevator" down to our heart is a wonderful starting place for plugging in, and it is a much more powerful setup for presence than staying in our brains. In fact, our brains can't take us to presence (I tried that, too).

There are uncountable people throughout time who have given us really great insights and techniques to finding the peace. The universal attribute pretty much always seems to involve silence. But let me be clear here: while I think silence is key, getting blissy hasn't always meant hear-a-pin-drop stillness all around me. I have had some of my most intense "A-ha!" moments while riding my bike in traffic, frying bacon for my family (very surprising for a vegetarian of thirty years), and walking to the store.

What we are doing while intending to open to stillness is not terribly important because **stillness is not about what's going on outside of us**.[57] I remember sitting wordlessly and stiff as a board at a beautiful Zen center in Northern California, a place perfectly set up for finding peace. Sadly, I had so much brain bustle going on that I never experienced a speck of bliss; in five lo-o-o-o-ng hours of talkless, cross-leggedness, not one miniscule moment of real peace popped up. I did, however, feel sharp pains in my back, cramping, prickly tingles in my leg, and intense yearnings for a tissue, as I spent the mini-eternity reviewing my frustration over numerous irksome details in my life at the time. I literally *ran* out of the center when the "evening of peace" was over!

Experience allows me to happily report that such self-chatter can be quelled with a little practice and a lot of intention. I have (mostly) learned

---

57 *Nothing* is about what's going on "outside" of us—I think the projector, screen, and editor are all inside us—but that's for another conversation!

how to achieve inner quiet when I focus and let go.[58] Mostly. For example, after a group meditation at a more recent conference, the organizer apologized for the intrusive leaf-blower commotion during the just-finished fifteen minutes of group silence. On that particular day (it is not always the case), I must have found my quiescent core because I had absolutely no idea what he was talking about! Outside noise—what outside noise? [59]

Such stillness really *can* happen once we consciously invoke it. For me, the most challenging aspect of experiencing silence has nothing to do with landscape maintenance—or any other exterior source, for that matter. It is usually my own proclivity for random *internal* distraction (important stuff, like what if I miss a deadline, or wondering if my dentist appointment is next Wednesday or Thursday) that prevents me from silently plugging in. And not only have I been known to distract myself *during* my period of silence, but after distracting myself from stillness, I have often been known to self-berate for not being able to find the stillness. What a silly, tautologically impossible thing to do! And yet...

God calls you and you do not hear,
for you are preoccupied
with your own voice.

—*A Course in Miracles*,
T-13.V.6:6

---

58 I know, those two concepts seem oddly out of step, but they are the closest words available to point to what I *really* mean.
59 Again, I'm sharing my experiences to *clearly* establish that even the most ridiculously talky and unfocused of us can achieve inner silence.

To keep my quiet connection on track—and for me, at least, this is a case where practice makes perfect—I engage a technique I've used in some of my best parenting moments. Most who live in the company of children have discovered "redirecting" to be a far more intelligent and effective tool for success than yelling like a banshee and making everyone feel like a big piece of poop. It's the same with plugging in. If I set my intention to clear my head (this can take place while seated peacefully, making dinner, or teaching a fifteen-and-a-half-year-old how to drive a stick shift: it does not matter!), and thoughts galore insist on pushing their way between my ears, I don't feel anxious or irritated at myself anymore. I just redirect those uninvited thoughts gently along and go back to plugging in. It's OK if I have to do that fifty-seven times during one sitting. That just gives me fifty-six chances to buff up my focus muscles!

I know, so submerged are we in electronicals, news, and background noise, that chosen silence can feel uncomfortably foreign at first. But it is glorious and worth attending to. As Rumi shared, "Silence is the language of God; all else is poor translation." So whatever way I plug in—peanut butter or jelly—I definitely invite silence.[60] You may think that's asking too much, given, well, life on planet Earth, but I'm not actually talking about the impracticality of trying to control all the outside cacophony. That would be futile! I mean the quiet we can create for ourselves in any given instant, mostly by *deciding* to experience it internally.

"Still listening" can happen in all sorts of ways. Sometimes my quietude consists of taking a walk and just thanking the trees, flowers, and birds. (Recently I came surprisingly close to a coyote and felt very thankful to have met his beautiful, clear eyes!) Other times I sit quietly on my living-room sofa, my unceasingly loving dogs rolled

---

60 I like to think of the silence as a spiritual amniotic fluid, keeping me safe and nourished as I grow.

up beside me. As often as I can, I meditate with friends and feel the amplification from time spent together in shared noiselessness. One way is not more "right" than the other, any more than salted caramel ice cream is absolutely, positively better than melon gelato. It's really all about what I'm in the mood for—what works best at any given time by holding an *intention* for silence (and as we've seen, that might even involve washing rice!).

Now that we have the main component, silence, out there, let's get back to the peanut butter. In the next exercises, I offer one kind of PB for those of us who generally like what's going on around us and another for those of us who aren't so thrilled with this phase in our lives. Again, one version is not better than the other; everything that's popping up for us now is simply a result of what we've felt before (and thus made true for us). But I've learned that emotions have their own directional momentum. So if you are generally happy-ish, finding your way to "happier" feels true and possible because you were already pointed that way. If, however, you are (metaphorically speaking) living in Yellville, Arkansas, trying to feel your way to a zip code in Happy, Texas, might seem too far to go in one trip.[61] In that case, I've found it best not to attempt that long journey till later.

So to recap, the difference in the following exercises is simply one of granularity. If you're living in general joy, it probably seems more realistic to get specific about joyful things. Head to Peanut Butter Plug-In #1. If happy for no reason tends to show up only sporadically for you—like every sixth Tuesday afternoon or so—then it might be more helpful for you to start by plugging in to more general feelings, ones that can feel true to you at this moment.

---

61 However, I do believe in miracles, so, what the heck, if you are living in Weedpatch, California, but totally—inside and out—believe it's possible to get to Joy, Illinois, in one intention, then definitely create that for yourself!

**EXERCISE 8A: Peanut Butter Plug-In #1
(Happy Residents)**

GO FOR IT!

1. When you wake up, set your timer for a whopping ten minutes of intending a joy-filled day. *Joy is the truth about you anyway, so it's not like you are asking for something you don't deserve.* You're pretty much just remembering who you are.

2. For about three-ish minutes, review the specific activities you have lined up, and imagine them—*feel* them—being *wonderful* experiences. Mentally go through events you know are on your calendar for the day. If you have a planned meeting with a coworker or teacher toward whom you generally experience negativity, imagine and feel that interaction going fabulously well. Imagine laughing, and enjoying yourself during the engagement. If your day is filled with menial tasks,[62] feel that you do them with as much enthusiasm as if your overall happiness depended on it (because, from a bigger perspective, it does). Has the repairman blown you off for days, and your broken what's-it really needs to be fixed? Send him Love and gratefulness, imagining how delightful it is to use your what's-it again. (Then don't be surprised if he calls you back when the ten minutes are up!)

3. Don't set up anything too specific in your brain. Just imagine the "happiness of the happiness" you are intending.

4. After you've done that, imagine light coming from your heart and filling everything you've just seen. Just stay in the light for the rest of your plugging-in session. If you

---

62 I don't believe anything is "menial" when it comes to our attitudes. Washing dishes joyfully can do just as much to bring us to a higher state as speaking at the UN, running a company, or…

start thinking, simply take the elevator down to your heart space again! It's fine and normal.

5. When the alarm chimes, practice feeling grateful for a really wonderful day, as if you are at the end of it, gleefully reminiscing.

6. Have a great plugged-in day.[63]

EXERCISE 8B: Peanut Butter Plug-In II (Yellville Residents)[64]

GO FOR IT!

1. When you wake up, set your timer for a whopping ten minutes of intention toward a joy-filled day. *Joy is the truth about you, anyway, so it's not like you are "asking" for something you don't deserve.* You're pretty much just remembering who you are.

2. For about three-ish minutes, review the stuff that's going right in your life—or, if there's not enough for you to find in your life that seems worth celebrating at the moment, think of things that are going right in the world. For example, as I write this, I can look out and see the prettiest sunrise. My son told me the sunrise yesterday was so glorious that all the bus-riding kids on their way to school shouted about it. Now, if grade schoolers—folks who frequently forget to brush their teeth or bring home their lunch boxes—can break free from their oblivion to

---

63 OK, so I'm not ignoring the irony of having to plan ahead to be present. But really, think of it as a retraining. Once you have reoriented your perceptions, you will not need to plan for happiness. You can just find it at Will Call when you get "there."

64 Only temporary residents of a less-than-joyful place. You'll soon have the momentum to move uptown, so to speak!

notice a sunrise, certainly we adults can muster that level of awareness.

If you are reading this, it is likely you live in a spot on the globe that is not experiencing war or anarchy. That's good! You can read, I assume. How lucky is that! Literacy pretty much puts the world at your fingertips... you can go *anywhere* in a book! Do you have a place to live? Think about how great it is to have a safe place to sleep at night. Do you have a job? OK, even if you hate your boss and are grossly underpaid in your opinion, you can appreciate the fact that you have employment, which means you probably have food to eat on a regular basis. Just devote a bit of marveling to the really good stuff you forgot to notice before, while you were putting so much of your attention on the other than good (like your crummy car—oh, wait, you have a car! Or how the gal who cuts your hair is *always* late—oh, wait, you have hair!)[65]. Try to think of Dr. Wiseman's lucky photo-finding research.

3. Now breathe in and out deeply two or three times, and let even the newfound gratitude fall away. As you breathe in, imagine moving upward so you can get an even better view of the good stuff when you come out of this exercise. Relax. Breathe. Enjoy.

4. After you've climbed a little higher, imagine light filling you and everything you've just seen, and stay in the light for the rest of your plugging-in session. If you start thinking, gently blow the thoughts away. It's fine.

5. When the alarm chimes, practice feeling grateful for the really wonderful day you created. Imagine you are at the

---

65 Yet another disclaimer: when you are thinking of reasons to feel lucky, please try to have your gratitude be independent of anyone else's misfortune.

end of the day, and you've appreciated where you live, your job, your town, and the other parts of your life.

6. Have a great plugged-in day.

7. If, as you go through your day, you start feeling the peace slip away, recall the feelings of all the light and appreciation you created for yourself only hours before.

Maybe you still don't think you have time for something that isn't "absolutely necessary." I get it. Stillness can feel pointless in a world where we all have so much to "do." At periods in my life, I believed I didn't have time to plug in because the book I'd just read/class I'd just taken/expert lecturer I'd just heard suggested that to be effective, I should find stillness for twenty minutes. Daily, while sitting up straight. Twice every day was even better. Oh, and meditating at the exact same *times* each day was suggested as optimal. Uh-huh. In many phases in my life, all that seemed too Herculean to even ponder! So I simply did not.

When I had my first child—probably the time in my life I could have used plugging in the most—I couldn't fathom being organized enough to plug in my slow cooker full of dry beans, let alone sit quietly, plugging myself in to "do nothing." Now, of course, I know differently, and *plugging in is what makes everything else flow more smoothly.* And now I also know that rules around plugging in are like recipes: suggestions about what is delicious to someone else, and possible ideas—jumping-off points—for me. The only thing that really matters is to, well, just do it…in whatever way works best at the time.

Given my long-term and multitudinous attempts at centering, I should be a wise and inspiringly unflappable mystic by now, radiating bliss with every exhale ("Yes, young grasshopper…"). Ahem, while that is definitely not yet the case, I *do* wake up rather happy most every day, and I *do* use my Crock-Pot without even the teensiest remnant of intimidation.

So what changed, really? As with a surprising number of things in my life, I'm pretty sure I was making plugging in too difficult. Trying too hard. I didn't understand the value of surrender. Understanding surrender has been incredibly helpful to plugging in, whether peanut butter or jelly style.

What I've experienced is that bliss is more about letting go than "getting there." It's more like just opening a clenched fist than getting out the binoculars, a book, or a map to seek some perfect path or prescribed meditation style. It really, really is about surrender.

Ah, but surrendering is such an unpopular notion in many cultures, and surely in my own. Where I live, the bumper stickers encouraging that we "Secede" are *not* actually kidding, and monuments to the Civil War still populate the state-capitol grounds. Surrender don't come easy in these here parts.

However, the surrender I'm talking about has absolutely nothing to do with loss or sacrifice. It is about connecting, trusting, and not clinging to my little ideas about what should happen. Big Love knows far better than little me. So despite my years of insistence to the contrary, by surrendering my small ideas to bigness, my worries to peace, and my fears to Love, happiness has (largely) found its way home.

Basically, I stopped trying to hog the driver's seat.

My elegant, kind, and centered friend Jennifer is a true expert at surrender and serves as a constantly amazing example for me. I have always felt that if I just worked a little harder, tried a little more, I could "do it," whatever "it" was. Enthusiasm and determination are good things, certainly! But in my case, most times I was just building a dam of not-havingness with all my effort and force. I wasn't very good at allowing grace to flow. Jennifer truly does hand it over to wall-to-wall Love, and she finds peace in the letting go. She has inspired me more times than I can number.

So now, rather than limiting plugging in to a certain way, at a certain time, with a certain planned outcome—like attaining enlightenment before my book-club meeting—I find it very worthwhile to open myself up in silence to Love's possibilities, which are all around us all the time. It feels like such a relief to know that there's not really any place to go to "plug in." And, even more freeing, to realize I don't need a laundry list of things to "pray for."

As I've mentioned (and will probably continue to mention because it's one of the main points of this book!), we can plug in right here, right now, mostly by deciding to be open to Love. No zafu necessary. I was bonked on the head by this realization one late night after finishing the truly delightful book *Eat, Pray, Love.* The extremely talented writer and thinker, Elizabeth Gilbert, meandered through Italy, India, and Indonesia to find her bliss. How awesome would that be? I went to bed ruminating over the constraintlessness of my previously free-as-a-bird-life, when I could (and did) take classes, attend meditation retreats, and travel whenever and wherever I wanted, bank-account permitting. Nobody else's laundry, schedule, or homework to keep me from reaching a higher level. "Ahh," I thought as I dozed off, "if I only had time to be spiritual again..."

I woke up to a thunderously loud voice. Well, not a "voice," exactly, but if words could form sensations in my head, that's how they often express themselves to me...Anyway, this head-voice vibrated loudly inside me, so as not to remain ignored, declaring, *"Your children are your daily devotionals, and your home is your ashram."*[66]

---

[66] An ashram, a spiritual retreat center, is one of the places Elizabeth Gilbert went to find her peace.

Oh.

That message did wonders to help me surrender to the never-actually-left-me truth. I'd gone to bed dwelling wistfully on the spirituality "out there" when really, *everything I needed to get to higher ground was surprisingly smack-dab in the middle of consistently unflushed toilets, sleep deprivation, and the inescapable schmutz of motherhood.* I had to laugh at myself: for so long, I'd been *striving* to meditate my way into centeredness, or wishing for a more ideal, balanced scenario, only to realize that my own best teachers for Love and being in the moment were generously sharing their wisdom under my very same roof, all the while wearing Bob the Builder underwear![67]

⟳

**You are exactly what God had in mind
when he made you.**

—FATHER GREGORY BOYLE

⟳

Speaking of schmutz, let's return to the jelly part of plugging in; that quick calling forth of bliss. Some of my favorite books[68] assert that merely saying a word or phrase can help immediately realign us with our truth. Rather than peace depending on us to create it, it is always vibrating all

---

67 I have no doubt that we each learn what and when we are supposed to, according to our own allowing. Nobody else will ever be, have, do, or get what I am supposed to be, have, do, or get. Elizabeth Gilbert's way of learning is perfect for her. (And I'm so thankful she continues to generously share it with us!)

68 There are four great books, so far, channeled by the beautifully humble and inspiring Paul Selig: *I Am the Word, The Book of Love and Creation, The Book of Knowing and Worth,* and *The Book of Mastery.*

around us, just awaiting our awareness. In *I Am the Word*, Paul Selig writes that by pronouncing, "I am the Word," we can align to our higher selves. We are "always an aspect of the Creator," he tells us, but being lined up to that big truth depends on our availability. If we are mired in chronic negative thinking (doubt, anger, fear, resentment—call it what you will) or just can't let go enough to really surrender, for example, we are temporarily out of sync with our innate perfection; we are not lining up with Love. What the decree "I am the Word" or "I am Word" accomplishes is to call us back to our deep-down truth, without a lot of extraneous chitchat.

Selig's *The Book of Knowing and Worth* offers another wonderful phrase, also based on remembering that we are really *all* Big Love: "I know who I am. I know what I am. I know how I serve." This all might sound a little simplistic *until you try it*. I have found amazing clarity and a whole different level of "being" in the world since I started incorporating those mindful maxims into my dailyness. If I start to feel stressed about something, attempt to "improve" a situation, or even just as I begin a meditation, I simply recall my truth using those phrases, or something very similar. (Remember, miracles don't need to take much time.) These types of phrases make awesome jelly!

Those may not be your best "tuning fork" phrases, but you can probably come up with something that resonates with you (after all, words are just symbols of symbols!). For me, having special wisdom watchwords that invite me to recall my ability to find joy and surrender in every moment has been nothing short of miraculous!

Speaking of significant phrases, this is probably a good place to mention TM—Transcendental Meditation—and *Lectio Divina*. People don't generally pack them in the same trunk, but having benefited similarly from the wisdom watchwords in each technique, I want to highlight their comparable merits. Besides, I am related to people who prefer more of a system to get "there" than freewheeling it with Love thoughts—or, eegads, *no* thoughts!—and these are a bit more "systemish." TM is an awesome form of meditation in which one is offered a mantra—a Sanskrit "sacred utterance"—and internally replays that word as a meditative anchor. I love how the process is all about ease: no forcing necessary. No trying to actively block out other thoughts. It's as if the mantra politely says, "This seat is taken," to those random ideas that so frequently threaten to sneak into our mindfulness movie. TM is also amazing in its research that backs up the power of meditating. Multitudes of TM studies point to benefits ranging from reduced crime in a community to reduced blood pressure in individual bodies. I practiced TM for many years and found it extremely, hugely, remarkably helpful.[69]

My interpretation of *Lectio Divina*[70]—Latin for "sacred reading"—is similar to TM in that it invites a "sacred utterance" to lead you into peace. *Lectio*[71] is different in that you can discover a new word or phrase each time you practice. Actually, what I've experienced is that the phrases find me! If I am seeking an answer to something, I have been stunned by what "shows up" for me to read "coincidentally." So I read a phrase or word, savor it, and, as Saint Benedict suggested, listen with the "ear of my heart." *Lectio Divina* is another great way to start the day, and it can be done quickly, or luxuriated in over any length of time. Peanut butter *or* jelly!

WHEN THE RUBBER HITS THE ROAD
(OR, IN THIS CASE, WHEN THE HEAD HITS THE FLOOR)

Had I only realized the power of the jelly plug-in sooner, I probably never would have experienced the Unfortunate Buddha Head Incident.

---

69 It is a practice that recommends two twenty-minute sessions daily. While the regularity is a success factor, it also might intimidate people and keep them from diving in.

70 *Lectio Divina* is an ancient Christian monastic practice that involves reading and contemplating Bible scriptures. Wisdom comes from any number of places, however, and I've found *Lectio* to be powerful, regardless of the written source.

71 Here is another difference: a TM teacher provides people with a TM mantra, generally at a cost. With *Lectio*, we can trust the universe to provide whatever phrase we need. The universe gets "paid" with all the happier vibes we send out!

It happened not too long after I "heard" about my real daily devotionals. Apparently to test my memory and resolve, my sons were wrestling upstairs...perilously close to an antique table I loved. I asked them to stop, reminding them how "It always ends with someone crying."[72] The next thing I heard was *thud-kerflump*, followed by an unidentifiable wobbling noise. Nobody was crying yet—hooray—but when I ran up to find out what happened, I witnessed the head of a beautiful terra-cotta Buddha, previously resting on said loved table, wobbling down the hall toward me.

I looked at my silent, wide-eyed children and the table that was now a dangling tripod, and *I* began to cry. This was a new twist on the crier, and my children were enlightened enough to note the ironic ridiculousness of Mom losing her equanimity over a broken clay Buddha and an old table. We can laugh about it now, but at the time, the Buddha Head Incident was solid proof of how I let my underwear get knotted by forgetting peace in the moment.

Were such an incident to occur today, I'd like to think I would remember how to call forth peace immediately. (Luckily, my children remain willing to help me try to practice calling upon that peace on a regular basis.) I definitely find that the more I plug in—the more I point my thoughts in the direction of centeredness—the less my equanimity rolls down the hall.

EXERCISE 9: I Declare! (A Jelly Plug-In)

GO FOR IT!

1. About the time you start your day—when you are just putting your feet on the ground, pouring your coffee, or heading out the door—declare for yourself that you'll be taking your peace with you *everywhere* you go today. Really, stop for about a nanosecond, and confirm that plan. Claim it.

---

72 Hmmm, that wouldn't be a form of priming, would it?

2. To punctuate that intention, throw in a word or phrase that will help you recall your plan. Here are a few more possibilities:
   * Amen (It means "so be it.")
   * Peace is right here, right now.
   * Everything is awesome.[73]
   * Yo, self, remember your radness!
3. Should an "unfortunate incident" occur, threatening to drop-kick your declaration for peace to another continent, just take a breath and remember peace. Call peace back with your power of intention. Feel the peace. Keep breathing until you deeply remember your radness. Now, cement it with your phrase of choice.
4. Go about your day as if nothing can crush your calm because now that you have *chosen* to be peaceful and have actively *invited* and *expected* peace, it will be there for you. And that *is* awesome!

Here's the bottom line: it's extremely valuable and enriching to meditate and/or pray regularly and frequently—it takes us home—but if we don't yet think we have time to do that, we can always bring more awareness and joy to the things we do regularly. Eckhart Tolle advises that we "become conscious of being conscious." What my children-shaped devotionals actively reinforce is that *bliss is amplified and fortified by being centered during the everyday stuff.* If I can do my laundry and respond to in-house demolitionists with the same equanimity I experience while attending an awesome, away-from-the-world retreat, or rambling through a gloriously invigorating redwood forest, or sitting wordlessly in my favorite bedroom chair, then I am

73 For those of you who have not enjoyed to *The Lego Movie* fourteen times, as my youngest son has, you may not be familiar with the song "Everything Is Awesome." I know it is meant mockingly, but when my son sings it, he dances with joy and really feels that everything is awesome. Amen!

finally living what I was reading about in all those books I've highlighted with my trusty yellow highlighter!

So I practice sitting quietly as frequently as I can, *and* I try to focus on peace and joy in the normal moments of life. It's a mutually reinforcing thing.

Mindfulness amid Materialism

Because there is so much attention on the Law of Attraction these days, I can't address silence without also speaking to what we can help create in silence. I definitely believe that we attract what we focus on, but focusing to *just* acquire a better car or a designer purse seems quite cart-before-the-horseish. It's not the very best use of what we call time. *Plugging in for stuff's sake only gets us more stuff, not necessarily more bliss.*

Bookstore shelves are lined with popular instruction manuals revealing the formulas for "having it all" by manifesting X, Y, and/or Z into our reality. Visualize. Write down affirmations. Incant "financial abundance," "a great job," or whatever seems lacking as our daily reverb. I completely understand where those authors are coming from, and I agree with many of them, to a point. *Of course* we can't collapse the wave function of possibilities without first adding our expectation to a possibility! And there's not a ding-dang thing wrong with stuff. Materiality is just energy densified. It is neutral.

It's our attachment to—and getting so totally sidetracked by—stuff that boots us out of the joy spot. Again, plugging in for stuff's sake only gets us more stuff, not more bliss. And most of the "manifesting" books I find act like stuff is the goal. They often leave out the part about plugging in first.

Plugging in with "stuff" as the goal is like being invited to Maria's house for dinner when her darling (exactly-how-we-pictured-Italian-grandmother) mother is in town, and not eating. Sure, I'd be at the table, but I'd miss so much deliciousness! (And, believe me, *nobody* would want to miss Nonna's gnocchi!)

Maria and Nonna

By intending something without first plugging in, we will probably miss something bigger.[74] Say my family is having a reunion in Iowa, so I'm busy affirming for the bus fare to Des Moines. I write down fifty times a day, "I have enough bus money to get to Des Moines. I have enough bus money to get to Des Moines." So when Uncle Ralph calls to tell me he's generously sending me bus fare, I think I really have found the secret to getting all the stuff I want. Wow, wasn't that *exactly* what I'd been affirming?

Well, but what if the universe had in mind the equivalent of a global tour via private jet? My manic, mantric insistence that I take the bus would have left me blind to possibly more exciting (and more comfortable!) options. Certainly what little ol' me can dream up is far less grand or fabulous than what Universal Mind can imagine and create. So why settle?

Somehow, though, the idea that *I* know much better about eternal fabulousness, or even general good stuff than the Omniscient Creative Being, has been a tough concept for me to release as I change my mind to a bigger truth. (Right—as if I could imagine, all by myself, making such stunning miracles as my children[75], a butterfly wing, or my favorite Adirondack waterfall!) For years I said my prayers as if I had some insights that Universal Intelligence may have, somehow—inadvertently of course—missed. My ego and I just weren't able to surrender to the idea that we didn't know what was best!

---

74 You get that I'm speaking of "bigger" in metaphorical terms, right? I don't think our limited perspective gives us a true take on "bigger." Yet.

75 Or the Love that came with them! I was shocked when my oldest son arrived on the planet, introducing me to a Love I had never before fathomed.

⟨⁓

**Our prayers should be for blessings
in general, for God knows best
what is good for us.**

—SOCRATES

⟨⁓

This realization struck me like a two-by-four one day when I read a prayer request that instructed us to begin praying like this: "Almighty God, please help so-and-so do such-and-such." *Thwack!* Like the Big Guy—almightiness notwithstanding—missed a problem in our part of town and needed a friendly tip-off from yours truly. Considered through those goggles, prayers that begin with our insights *to* God seem a little, well, arrogant, don't they?

Such prayers also imply that God's Love is variable. And to confirm that Universal Greatness might not always be Loving, there are all those nasty reports of a "vengeful God" (famine, pestilence, lakes that burn with fire and sulfur—that sort of thing).[76] With all the tales of God-generated get-evenness, *of course* it seems unwise to ask such a random and punitive dude for a favor and then mutely sit on the sidelines, hoping for the best. What if this particular request of yours is His chance to get even for that time you set off the fire alarm in eighth grade during finals? Or worse? No, not steering a vindictive guy with lots of dirt on us would be pure idiocy on our part. Right?

Nope. Infinite Love does *not* change. Ever. And it is always maximal. *We* are the variable aspect of this equation! And God is certainly not

---

[76] "Vengeful" is not, however, a word I use to describe the God I know. Love doesn't leave room for getting even—or even getting mad—because Love has no opposite!

spiteful! Love is available—ready and waiting for us—from our Source 24/7, eternally. How much Love we allow in is always the issue.

So, what I've slowly realized is that my "please" part of plugging in works best in a sentence like "Please help me listen better." My intentions now come more in the form of requests to understand, be receptive, and welcome more Love and wisdom. I am less likely these days to ask that amazing Infinite Mind for some *thing* than for a new attitude about that thing. "Please help me feel total Love, abundance, and joy in my new job" is a phrase I now find more helpful for plugging in than "Please let me get a forty-five percent increase in salary during my performance review on the twenty-third." I am constantly learning to trust and remember that the power of Love, permeating everywhen, has it covered.

⌒⌒⌒

Imagine the universe beautiful and just and perfect.
Then be sure of one thing: the Is has imagined it
quite a bit better than you have.

—Richard Bach

⌒⌒⌒

When our hearts speak to us from that silent space of prayer or meditation—when we are actually *listening*—we are often motivated to action or intention. In other words, *after* aligning with our inner source, we can effectively deal with the outer stuff. Jesus talked about this as "seeking first the kingdom of God." Once we have found our connection—our inner kingdom—we can better know where to "go" for the "everything else to be added" to us.[77] Insights we garner from the perspective of Love are surely gifts from our Higher Connection. So when we plug in and

---

77 Matthew 6:33.

align ourselves to our true joy that's waiting to be remembered (like those sunglasses on top of our heads), we can access more goodness than we'd be able to come up with on our own. *From the place of inspired peace, where we are truly listening, we can be or do anything.*

With this perspective, we can approach an understanding that our distracted individual intellect is incapable of grasping. When I am plugged in, I can ask questions and, through some form of quietness, receive answers I know are good for my soul. Intentioning through Love-kindled intuition is sacred. Intentioning via our ego, our non-plugged-in selves, simply misses the mark.

⟢⟶

There are two kinds of people:
those who say to God,
"Thy will be done,"
and those to whom God says,
"All right, then, have it your way."

—C. S. Lewis

⟢⟶

Perhaps the reason *not* adding our own two cents seems so difficult is that we hardly know how to release our firmly clutched ideas of right and wrong, good and bad (which, by the way, are always based on our assumptions and perceptions from the past). Who wants to seem wishy-washy or even "unrealistic" in this world of big, loud, and incessantly shared opinions? Most of TV's reality shows seem to be about judging who is good and who is bad (according to a small group of "experts," "judges," and "fashion police"). Who merits a trip to the finals in Las Vegas, and who deserves a condemningly loud "X"? Contrary to very popular and emphatic opinion, life is not an either/or proposition.

Allowing things to flow through us without labeling or arguing for or against them—surrendering—is a skill seldom practiced these days (and not at all encouraged by social media). We all so unthinkingly, so reflexively, label something, that it doesn't occur to us that *everything doesn't need a label*. What if we just enjoyed it as is? What if we flowed right along without stopping to judge? In philosophical terms, this is called not investing in duality (more on that in the "Kale versus Cookie Dough" chapter).

Besides, if we look back at what happens when we cling to right/wrong and good/bad, we find that our typically human responses—often religion-motivated, like the Crusades, Inquisition(s), Jihads, witch hunts, Aztec sacrifices—have added a heap of extra pain to our earthly experience. If we could just remember how to leave out our smaller ideas and condemnations, we would allow lots more room for Infinite Wisdom to express greater-than through us (no labels, rights, or wrongs necessary!).

To help find a place of silent, nonjudgy clarity, I offer this general formula that works well for me. It's just a variation on *the* theme, but then, they all are, really!

EXERCISE 10: Clear the Decks

GO FOR IT!

First of all, please remember that this is just what works for me. You may very well be able to use this method "off the shelf," or it may lead you elsewhere equally valuable and important. You can do this in a time "set apart," or when you suddenly remember as you're hopping out of your car to pick up the cat litter you've been meaning to get for three days.

1. Get quiet. We don't have to be in a monastery or get everyone out of the house. True quiet is not about what is going on *around* us. **Quiet is the power we carry with us 24/7** (we begin to access it by deciding to!).
2. Breathe. Oh, wait, we do that anyway...see how natural this is? So maybe a better instruction is to breathe while actually paying attention. No need to think. No need to "do." Let air flow in and out of your lungs, easily. "Watch" it go in and out.
3. If, two and a half breaths in, your brain starts shooting you thoughts like "Who's going to win Fantasy Football at work?" take another deep breath and let that thought flow...like water down a stream.
4. Keep breathing and just watch. No thoughts, no judgments.
5. Now add your deepest desire. You may assume it's having more money, but think about it a little more. That is a little, temporary wish compared to say, peace of mind (POM). Or permanent joy. Go deeper—you deserve more than that! If you proclaim your wish to be POM, that will cover all the other stuff, including worries about money you may have (because money is likely just one of the things to come between you and POM, or permanent joy).
6. Breathe in the joy, peace, or whatever it is you are claiming. We've all claimed other-than-joy for so long, that might feel silly or impossible. Stick with it. Call it yours. When you are done—however long it may be, because it doesn't matter—feel the POM go with you. (Now you can get the cat litter!)

In the Silence

There are many, many reasons to invite silence into our lives, not the least of which is that it helps us hear better. See better too. Technically, I'm not talking audiovisual here (though, certainly, that can happen). I'm referring to something much, much more. Silence invites what can be called "perceptual acuity." It can heighten our awareness of insights we may never have noticed before, helping to create space in our thinking for new information. *By being unnoisy, our normally muted intuition sings to us and informs us of all the good stuff we've been loudly ignoring.*

We may feel silly at first, listening to our "gut" or our "mere feelings," or suddenly finding that we really need to search our hearts instead of the Internet. But the more we listen and respond, the more we can know that the "still, small voice" is the most trustworthy source of really good information we will ever discover. And it is with us all the time! As Søren Kierkegaard said, "Praying is not listening to oneself speak but is about becoming silent and, in becoming silent, waiting, until the one who prays hears God."

So…spirituality/bliss/heaven is not a single-lane highway devoted to meditation and/or prayer when we are in a special place, at a special time, sitting a special way. *Ultimately, I hope to make my life one perpetual prayer.* Or more precisely, I'd like the silent bliss I feel while living life to *be* my perpetual prayer. We are all free to become the joy we want, even in the midst of what we don't want, and silence (prayer/meditation) is a really miraculous way to allow that!

I can hear a few of you now, exclaiming something along the lines of "Prayers are B?&%@$!" There are many who think prayer/meditation/sending positive energy is just a cop-out coping mechanism for people who *wish* they had answers. Maybe they're weak. Or maybe they're just plain stupid. I totally get it. Prayers—like their cousins, miracles—aren't always easy to touch for those of us expecting burning bushes or talking donkeys. So to help explain how truly powerful plugging in can be, I will lean once again on science. Head to the Internet right now (or your library, if you prefer) and look at the scientific research done on prayer and meditation. You will find study after study revealing that folks who plug in are just plain healthier than those who don't: they have increased levels of dopamine, more youthful appearances, less depression and anxiety, improved immune systems, reduced blood pressure and cholesterol levels, better memories, and so on. There are a lot of medically measurable improvements resulting from just being silent. Statistically, plugger-inners are healthier, *and* they live longer. Oh, and while they are living out their healthier lives, they also experience more peace. That does not seem like B?&%@$ to me.

MIT and Harvard researchers (among others) claim that those meditation benefits come from the fact that people who spend time plugging in are better able to control their alpha brain waves.[78] It's my bet that those waves don't just wiggle around in our bodies, bouncing back and forth between the sides of our skulls or inside our skin. It seems natural that such waves would emanate outward, beyond our bodies, doesn't it? Surely you've experienced waves emitted from people. We even talk about how people give off "good vibes" or "bad vibes." *Whether we are taking charge of them or not, our vibes are always radiating, and those vibes correlate directly to our consciousness.*

If the idea that we radiate waves seems hard to swallow, chew on this: we know that sound and light travel in waves, so why can't thoughts travel in waves?[79] Wait—*thoughts* traveling in waves? Not so sure about that last one? I know, the fact that thoughts travel in waves

---

78 These waves are measured by an electroencephalogram—an EEG—and have a frequency of 8 to 13 Hz.
79 Actually, I think *everything* is in wave form, but more on that another day.

is a proposition currently less scientifically demonstrable and certainly less well-measured than the other waves we learned about in fifth-grade science class.

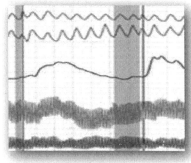

A polygraph

However, thoughts *can* get measured in waves: think about a lie detector. It waveishly graphs changes in heart and respiratory rate, blood pressure, and electrodermal activity (aka sweatiness) based on a person's responses to certain questions—his *thoughts*. The change in someone's "charge" (a body's electric potential) gets measured, confirming that **we actually create different vibrations depending on what we think about** (à la the treadmill). Polygraph testing is said to be between 98 and 99 percent accurate. So solid, in fact, that certain posts with the FBI and CIA necessitate polygraph tests for employment.

A book I've loved for decades, *The Secret Life of Plants* by Peter Tompkins and Christopher Bird, reveals how lie detectors can record thought waves. The transmission of human thought as a measurable "thing" is actually secondary to the book's idea that plants receive our thoughts and create their own waves in response. It highlights my point that we humans are dispatchers of detectable thought waves, so I'll share this example with you.

Way back in the 1960s, a man named Cleve Backster, who ran a polygraph training school, got curious one day and for some reason hooked his office palm tree up to his galvanometer. Imagine Backster's shock when the plant registered a response to his mere *thought* of lighting the plant on fire. Backster went on to conduct many more experiments, all of them yielding similar conclusions: human thoughts—though generally not perceived as physically palpable—flutter through our environment and create responses in unexpected ways. Even for nonwalking members of the planet, and even at tremendous distances.

So, although we did not learn this in school, it's a true fact: our thoughts—which we cannot see with our eyes—ripple out from us in wave-like fashion, influencing stuff we can see. Like plants. But surely, plants are not the only ones affected by our thoughts.

A wonderful example of how our thoughts affect the stuff around us comes from the work of Dr. Masaru Emoto. Dr. Emoto was a forward-thinking Japanese researcher who found surprising molecular changes in water due to words and thoughts (and their inherent, linked emotions). The shape of a water molecule can change in response to words? Yep. Here's how he demonstrated the power of thought to change matter. He wrote certain words on bottles filled with water—such as hate, Love, anger, and peace—froze the water, and photographed the ice crystals under high magnification. And those pictures are amazing. The water treated with "positive" thoughts is what we would consider beautiful. Not so the poor water that experienced unkind intentions. Really. I'm not kidding. I recommend Dr. Emoto's work and books as great visual inspirations.[80]

Expanding beyond bottled water, however, Dr. Emoto demonstrated the power of Love's intention to alter bigger bodies of water, like lakes! In 1999, some 350 people gathered around Japan's nasty, smelly Lake

---

80 Of course, there are people intent on debunking Emoto's work. To think that Love really has that much power can be frightening to those who have adamantly blocked such a possibility.

Biwa and sent it Love. The before and after pictures of the water's crystals are impressive. Before Love, the molecular structure of the water is globby and sludgy-looking. After Love, the structure is beautiful, symmetrical, and sparkling.

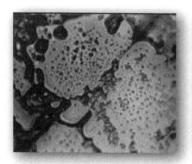 

© Office of Masaru Emoto, LLC

The picture on the left is Lake Biwa water before the prayer ceremony. The picture on the right is Lake Biwa water after the prayer ceremony. Big difference, right?

While I have not gathered hundreds lakeside to document for myself the veracity of Dr. Emoto's claims, I did undertake another of his experiments with impressive—and easily documentable—results. In a try-this-at-home kind of experiment, Dr. Emoto placed white rice in jars with water and directed different thoughts toward the jars. You can probably guess where I'm going with this. The rice that was treated kindly stayed pristine. Not so the "You fool!" rice (think dark and moldy). Lots of other curious experimenters have conducted this exercise as well, and you can find it mentioned many places on the Internet (search "rice experiment"). Or even better, try it yourself; all you need are glass jars, white rice (I used organic), water, time, and, most of all, intention.

I have to admit that when I conducted this experiment in my own kitchen, I had a very hard time purposefully sending mean thoughts to anything, already so strongly believing in the power of sent energy. But I tried it. I can't say my results were as impressively moldy as some others I've seen, but the un-Loved rice definitely turned brown, and my Love-recipient rice remained white. (For the colorful examples of my own rice experiment, please visit my website, KellyCorbet.com.)

Dr. Emoto believed in the power of the energy we all emit, and he understood that energy can be transferred through thought. He demonstrated what in Japanese is called *hado*. As Dr. Masaru explained it, *"Hado* is the intrinsic vibration pattern at the atomic level in all matter, the smallest unit of energy. Its basis is the energy of human consciousness." In Japanese, *hado* literally means vibration or motion.

BETTER TOGETHER

As demonstrated by Dr. Emoto, and many others, sending out a group intention for Love effects bigger waves than any person can manage solo.[81] Physics, helpfully, has a name for this phenomenon: "constructive interference." Interference is what happens when two waves get in each other's space. Basically, the principle goes like this: two waves, headed the same direction with the same frequency and phase, literally "amp" each other up to twice the wave either could manage alone. The two waves achieve what is called "linear super-position." If one thousand waves are vibing at the same amplitude, constructively interfering with each other, the amassed amplitude is one thousand times greater than that of a single wave! And so it goes with the plugging-in thoughts we send from our hearts together with others. The greater we can intensify thoughts, the "louder" they become.

---

81 This is not the case for those who have already mastered Love, like Jesus.

⌒

The Principle of Linear Superposition:
When two or more waves come together, the result
is the sum of the individual waves.

⌒

This evidence is partially why, as I mentioned earlier, I am a big fan of meditating with my friends and family. Not only is it a peaceful thing to do, but as science confirms, is it ever-powerful! We don't have to make a big production of it, either. For example, almost daily, my openhearted, very dear friend Melinda and I text each other with the code "MPN" for MediPray Now. We stop what we are doing (if it's appropriate), and spend five, ten, or twenty minutes in shared peace in different locations. If we get the chance, we meditate in the same room, but we don't wait for physical togetherness. We have both felt the energy shift when we MPN from different parts of town, or even in different countries[82]. On a less regular basis, I MPN with other dear friends. I like to think of it as amplifying Love.

Of course, Jesus—who was wayyyyy ahead of his time on anything related to Love—told us all this ages ago, though he didn't find it necessary to pull in the concept of linear superposition. In Matthew 18:19-20, he said, "Again, I say unto you, that if two of you on earth agree about anything…that they shall ask, it shall be done for them of my Father which is in heaven. For where two or three are gathered together in my name, there am I in the midst of them." My translation of that passage is this: "If a few of you get together and plug in to your highest selves, your alignment will

---

82 We have also practiced lessons in *A Course in Miracles* simultaneously. Although it is a self-study course, practicing along with Melinda offered me quite a blessing.

help you remember your Love-centered truth. And from that space, my friends, there's just no limit!"

Those impressive researchers behind Transcendental Meditation (TM) in the United States have conducted quite a few studies on the positive effects of group meditation and intention. They even have their own term for what is, essentially, constructive interference: Super Radiance. I love that phrase! The TM folks have diligently charted and graphed their research projects over several decades and have recorded many statistically significant, impressive changes from group intention, including these:

* Reduced terrorism
* Reduced crime in an area
* Fewer suicides
* Fewer accidents and emergency calls
* Reduced alcohol consumption
* Decreased number of war-related deaths

Pretty impressive, huh? Naturally, this research is on a specific way to plug in—TM—and I'm very thankful for that. As you know, however, it is my view that a single style of plugging in is not the only way to bliss. Some plants like acid soil, while some like alkaline: growing and thriving can be done in all types of dirt! As Paul Selig writes, "There is no 'my way or the highway' in consciousness." I suspect that most TM teachers would agree with that statement.

The point of all this conscious thinking info is to underscore that every thought is like a little prayer, vibrating its way out into the universe with our intent (conscious or not). Every intentional group thought is like a tsunami. Either way, our prayer-thoughts ripple over people, plants, and events in ways that we can neither predict nor fully comprehend from a little perspective. But they are powerful, as any plant hooked up to a lie detector will be sure to confirm! *The energy we create through our thoughts affects the world around us, whether we are actively conscious of it or not. And, when we consciously emit thoughts together, the effects are even bigger.*

Imagine, then, what the world could look like if we could vibrate Love, all of us, at every moment! To quote John Lennon again, "You may say I'm a dreamer, but I'm not the only one."

CHAPTER 7

Connected

I celebrate myself,
And what I assume you shall assume,
For every atom belonging to me as good belongs to you.

—WALT WHITMAN

You are not a drop in the ocean.
You are the entire ocean in a drop.

—RUMI

"QUANTUM ENTANGLEMENT" IN THE PHYSICS lab deals with separated particles that, at one point, were physically, measurably connected. In repeatable outcomes that are oh-so-counter to our expectations, the particle halves *act* like they are sharing information as a whole unit, simultaneously, even when they are separated by immense distance! For example, when Particle A changes charge, its other far-away half, Particle B, changes too, at *exactly* the same time (which makes it "superluminous," faster than the speed of light, and that really messes with some famous physics theories).[83]

---

83 Einstein never quite bought into entanglement, famously calling it "spooky action at a distance."

Many physicists treat this entanglement stuff as a "special connection," between pairs of quantum somethings. With all due respect to those brilliant and creative minds,[84] I would add that particles are not the only things entangling; we are all entangled with each other[85] by virtue of our common consciousness.

When an electron vibrates,
the whole universe shakes.

—Eddington

By "consciousness," I mean our alignment with infinite intelligence— not the subjective "mine" or "yours" consciousness, but the collective, knowing conduit through which information abides and is shared. We are swimming (and walking and running and sleeping and dancing) in this intelligent energy field that invisibly binds us together, responding to our thoughts, and moreover, our *feelings*. You know what's coming, right? It's that Big Love that connects us (along with Particles A and B!).

I realize this idea can still be a bit difficult to fathom. It does not match what we expect to see. And judging by the seeming *consensus omnium*— the agreement of all—as Jung would say, we are still mostly searching for "proof" so that we can believe some cosmically connecting glueishness measurably exists. (And when we do find more evidence of a connection, I'm surprised at the outright anger such findings arouse.)

---

84 Who don't all agree with each other, by the way.
85 More than entangled, I believe we aren't even separate from each other, but until we can get past believing in everything we "see," let's work on the idea of connectedness from this angle.

One fascinating development comes from a series of experiments on water (what is it with water?) and other liquids conducted under Dr. Bernd Kröplin, first at the University of Stuttgart's Aerospace Engineering and Geodesy. He has since gone on to work independently from the university; publish a beautifully illustrated book on his findings, *World Drops*; and win the Körber European Science Prize.

Initially attempting to develop a "simple space medicine" for astronauts who didn't have access to a doctor while off exploring the cosmos, what Dr. Kröplin's team discovered using dark-field microscopy is stunning. The experiment I found particularly amazing proceeded something like this. The researchers invited a group of people to the university, poured several of them water from the same pitcher, and asked them to simultaneously place drops of water on individual microscope slides. The researchers then examined the water drops and discovered that water from the same initial pitcher, but dropped by *different* people from their individual water, assumed unique profiles under the microscope!

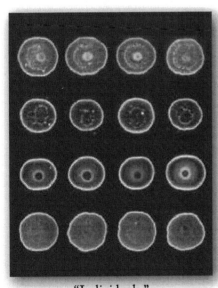

"Individuals,"
Copyright: Prof. Dr. Bernd Kröplin
World in a Drop/worldinadrop.com

Each row shows drops from a single experimenter. The rows look very similar in markings, shapes, and colors. Among the various columns, though, the drops from different water-dropping volunteers look remarkably varied. What could have caused that? Could it be that the energy a person emanates gets "remembered" or "embossed" in the water? Would that indicate a previously unnoticed connection between the water and the individual? How would the water have received the information if not for some sort of connecting medium through which that information could have been transferred?

In a place I consider very far from Germany in many ways— California—"connection" experiments have been conducted by the Institute of HeartMath, a visionary nonprofit dedicated to "help establish heart-based living and global coherence by inspiring people to connect with the intelligence and guidance of their own hearts." In the compelling documentary *I AM*, director Tom Shadyac examines just how HeartMath measures this connectedness. He does this by illustrating how his emotions affect live active cultures, aka yogurt, on a table in front of him. This creator of popular films like *Bruce Almighty*, *The Nutty Professor*, and *Ace Ventura: Pet Detective*, seats himself before a petri dish of yogurt that is equipped with an activity-measuring probe. To be clear, the probe is not touching Tom: it's touching the yogurt. Nothing about the yogurt is physically attached to Tom. Yet when he speaks of topics that activate in him a certain kind of energy (his ex-wife, his lawyer), the probe measures serious feedback! How could that happen if not for some "medium" through which responses could be measured?[86]

I experienced my own probe-free version of this phenomenon with my homemade kombucha.[87] We had hosted uninvited houseguests for quite a while, and I'd been resistant to their arrival in the first place. The longer they stayed in our home, the more my own equanimity stayed on vacation. By the end of their visit, when I discovered half-empty wine glasses, old cans of Diet Coke, and wet towels on my guest-room floor, my bitterness decided to override my ability to find Love.[88] My attitude and energy were definitely no secret to my much-loved fermenting kombucha. Very soon after the company had departed, it was time to stop the brewing process

---

86 I highly recommend this documentary. It is so well done and brings up some great points!
87 Kombucha is a fermented tea drink, a probiotic beverage filled with live active cultures.
88 I am not proud of this moment, but it was a good learning opportunity for me and my ego!

and enjoy a delicious glass of kombucha. This time, however, there was absolutely nothing "delicious" about it! It was bitter, bitter, bitter. Now, sometimes I've been known to let a batch of booch sit too long, in which case it can get a tad sour, but that is easily remediated by adding it to a subsequent sweeter, less-fermented batch. Unfortunately, it turns out that "bitter" is too hard to remediate—at least in kombucha—so I had to throw out the entire batch (something that has happened neither before nor since). While I am sorry I spent even a moment of my life being bitter—and inadvertently sharing my bitterness—it was an awesome educational accident.

While anecdotal evidence can often be extremely convincing, those who haven't experienced much beyond five of their senses can find it less than adequate. So, I will refer to "hard," measurable science, to share what those gifted scientists have to say about our connected reality. I footnoted Dr. William A. Tiller back in chapter 4, but now it's time to bring his bold ideas more fully into the spotlight. A professor emeritus from Stanford, Dr. Tiller founded the Institute for Psychoenergetic Science, an organization whose first mission is "to design and conduct careful laboratory experiments in the psychoenergetics area to reveal in quantitative detail how human consciousness interacts with the various energies and materials of physical reality as well as the higher dimensional aspects of our overall reality." To me, that indicates that they intend to make our invisible connectedness "believable" through measurable, scientific means.

He is up front about "consciousness"[89] being part of the equation, literally. In fact, he fearlessly adds consciousness to the world's most famous equation: $E = mc^2$, or, energy equals mass times the speed of light squared. What Einstein's incredibly famous but not completely understood equation tells us is that energy and matter are pretty much different forms of

---

89 His definition and use of consciousness is "a unique quality of nature that is ultimately convertible to energy (and thus mass), although it also conforms to the typical dictionary usage of being awake, aware, etc."

the very same thing. Energy is contained in matter, and matter is contained in energy; they are convertible. This finding was quite surprising, even to Einstein, given that most everyone previously believed that energy and matter weren't even related to each other.

While Dr. Tiller agrees that matter and energy are intrinsically related, he proposes that consciousness is required for the conversion. Dr. Tiller's version is this:

Mass ⇔ Energy ⇔ Information ⇔ Consciousness

Wow, a real numbers guy using an equation that includes consciousness...now we're getting somewhere! But wait, does his scientific way of including consciousness invite plugging in? Sure it does.

One of the experiments Dr. Tiller conducted to demonstrate his consciousness-including formula starred—can you guess?—water. This time, the goal was to change the pH level because pH is easily measured and not prone to wild natural fluctuations. As a sort of consciousness caddy, he used a very simple circuit, or "host device," he calls a UED, an Unimprinted Electrical Device. It looks like my TV remote without all the buttons. He called on experienced meditators (people who definitely knew how to find their connection to *connection*) to send their intention to two different UEDs. This intention-sending would then convert the UED into an IIED, an Intention Imprinted Electrical Device! As Dr. Tiller said:

Our working hypothesis is that the "unseen" does the *heavy* lifting in this cooperative process between dimensions; a necessary component to the overall creation event of converting a seemingly inanimate UED host device to a seemingly dynamic and intelligent IIED.[90]

---

90 This is from Dr. Tiller's awe-inspiring book *Psychoenergetic Science: A Second Copernican-Scale Revolution* (Walnut Creek, CA: Pavior Publishing, 2007), 51.

The plan was that one device would move a water sample *up* a full pH unit, and the other intention-embedded device would nudge the water's pH *down* one full pH unit. So, did this experiment essentially try to prove that intention—thoughts—can be gathered up, like marbles in some mechanical device, and stored? Looks like it did, because without the addition of chemicals (or any other "physical" interference), each IIED-exposed water sample changed according to the intention that had been sent its way. The pH went up in one, and down in the other, just as intended through "unseen" consciousness.

<hr />

There is no matter, as such.
All matter originates and exists only by virtue of a force which brings the particle of an atom to vibration and holds this most minute solar system of the atom together. We must assume behind this force the existence of a conscious and intelligent mind. This mind is the matrix of all matter.

—MAX PLANCK

<hr />

I do not mean to suggest that other esteemed scientists necessarily rejected consciousness as part of their vision; they just didn't do experiments that were so simple for our nontechnical brains to understand. David Bohm, the eminent physicist (and philosopher), put it this way: "We are all linked by a fabric of unseen connections. This fabric is constantly changing and evolving. This field is directly structured and influenced by our behavior and by our understanding."

And Sir James Hopwood Jeans (I am completely smitten by this guy) had this to say in a published interview from the London *Observer*:

I incline to the idealistic theory that consciousness is fundamental, and that the material universe is derivative from consciousness, not consciousness from the material universe...In general the universe seems to me to be nearer to a great thought than to a great machine. It may well be, it seems to me, that each individual consciousness ought to be compared to a brain-cell in a universal mind.

So, with this information from some really smart folks freshly holding our attention, it may be easier to rethink what we have held about our interconnectedness. What about conducting an intention experiment now?

EXERCISE 11: Gedankenexperiment

GO FOR IT!

Have you ever wondered what it would be like to think like a genius? Now's your chance. Einstein was famous for (among other things) enjoying a good a "thought experiment" or *gedankenexperiment*. He employed these to help him pursue an idea that may have been physically impossible (like chasing a light beam, the famous thought experiment he created when he was just sixteen years old).

This version of a thought experiment is super simple and requires no knowledge of advanced math or physics theories. It just asks that we use our centered intention to connect with something and have it "get physical" on us.

1. Imagine something you would like to show up for you in the next couple days. It could be silly or serious—either way works. The only requisite is that it not *seem* impossible

to *you* at the outset. For example, if you've never seen a $100 bill up close and personal, and you—literally—can't imagine holding one now, don't start with that. Not because it's "harder" to eke out of universal consciousness[91] but because you *think* it is. Instead, how about a $10 bill delighting you by suddenly showing up where you least expected it? Or invite something intangible, like your good friend who now lives in Buenos Aires (and you haven't talked to in a year and a half) giving you a call.

2. Get quiet and plug in. Take your focus to your heart, and breathe a few deep breaths. Now that you are in your connected space, imagine how fun it will be to find what you were asking for! *Feel* how great it feels to know you can do that!

3. Until it shows up, keep thinking how fun it is to expect (rather than creating a "This is dumb and nothing I want ever shows up for me anyway" type of intentioning).

4. We now know this:

Mass ⬌ Energy ⬌ Information ⬌ Consciousness

So when it arrives, you can delight in your knew scientific awareness of the connectedness you always had anyway!

5. Write down what came your way, if you remember. Writing helps me remember that I actually aligned myself enough to convert energy into mass through intention.

When I started writing this section, I practiced the exercise with my youngest son one night before bed. We "intentioned" a purple ball to show up for him the next day. When I asked him about a purple-ball sighting, he nonchalantly responded, "Oh, yeah, it was a purple football during PE,"

---

91 Universal Consciousness doesn't discriminate between "big" and "small" or "hard" and "easy." We are the ones who insist on all the labels.

and went on with his afternoon snack. He is not surprised when the world confirms his projections on a regular basis. Like most kids, he still largely remembers our universal connectedness.

Even though connectedness doesn't necessarily match what most of us believe we see (until now, of course!), it *does* match what we've all surely experienced. The "coincident" phone call, for example. "I was *just* thinking of you!" you tell your much-loved former boss when she calls for the first time in years. And what about learning a new word or hearing some crazy piece of random info for the first time, only to hear it again in proximate succession? (There's even a name for it: the Baader-Meinhof Phenomenon.) Swiss psychologist Carl Jung coined "synchronicity" for seemingly "acausal events."[92] Together with the brilliant, Nobel prize-winning physicist, Wolfgang Pauli, Jung spent years engaged in uncovering the invisible connection (they called it "psychic," as opposed to physical) between what could be explained tangibly, or at least "scientifically," and what simply could not. Pauli was forever trying to "find a new language that could make the hidden dimension in nature accessible to the intellect."

It has been my experience that the more aware we become of the field that unites us all, the more frequently we experience synchronicity (aka intuition, clairvoyance, and telepathy). But those are not the miracle. Those are just side effects of getting closer to our true selves and our connection to each other. What we can acknowledge, then, is the Love that makes them possible.

---

92 When "acausal events"—events for which we can find no "rational cause"—seem bigger than a phone call or a new concept, we tend to call them miracles!

CHAPTER 8

Rage, Resentment, and Forgiveness

⟵⟋

For every minute you remain angry,
you give up sixty seconds of peace of mind.

—RALPH WALDO EMERSON

As I walked out the door toward the gate that would lead to
my freedom, I knew if I didn't leave my bitterness and
hatred behind, I'd still be in prison.

—NELSON MANDELA

WHILE JOYFUL SURE FEELS BETTER than bitter or bummed, few of us are able to maintain that state at all times...yet.[93] However, it is never helpful to get mad at ourselves for getting mad (or sad, or disappointed, or...) at someone or something else. *It's what we do with those bummed emotions that either helps us grow or keeps us stuck*. If we treat our resentment like a favorite pet, showing it to everyone wherever we go and feeding it until it's the size of a woolly mam-

---

93 Well, maybe the Dalai Lama and Pope Francis—and certainly my boxer dog—are able to constantly resonate peace, but they are notable exceptions for now!

moth, it will be a hard thing to squeeze past. Sure, we can (potentially) garner piles of support and sympathy for being "wronged," but how does that really help us be happy in the long run?

Of course, I *never* advocate stuffing sentiments or pretending we don't feel what we feel. That would be counterproductive because, given their whack-a-mole proclivity, suppressed emotions like to show up elsewhere, disguised as ulcers, stiff necks, or worse. I am *not* suggesting that we sing at the top of our lungs with make-believe mirth after our dog dies. Nor am I advocating that we "think" our way out of what we are experiencing as real sadness. No, no, no! If we do that, we are just adding to the duality of things, making a bigger pile of good/bad to have to surmount! If I'm mad, I let myself be mad…I just think it's important not to spend a honkin' chunk of my time fuming when I might as well be peaceful, laughing, or having fun.[94] It is *my* life, after all, and do I really want to waste it being indignant, hateful, and/or bitter? (Believe me, I've already devoted enough precious minutes of my life to those unfruitful pursuits!)

So, without faking happiness or bulldozing feelings into our cells, how do we handle what, at this stage, seem to be natural "bad" emotions?[95] My best way is to respond to them as if they are young children and do what works so well with toddlers who are about to have a tantrum: distract them. I'm not being flippant. Really, just think back to times you've witnessed this strategy work so incredibly well. Say a two-year-old wants a certain kitchen utensil very, very badly. However, the object of fascination happens to be a pointy corkscrew that, if it didn't poke out one or both of her eyes, would certainly pinch her little fingers. You wisely intuit that this is not a sound combo and ask her to release it. She's not happy about letting go and begins to respond; quietly at first, but soon she's up to a high-pitched howl. This is precisely when you introduce her to the doll

---

94 The more time we spend plugging in, the less time we naturally tend to fume. It's a fabulous side effect.

95 Disclaimer: they seem natural now only because our focus is not on our bliss.

(or toy, cookie, or anything she finds delightful) on the counter! Isn't she cute? What color dress should we put on her? Would she like this one or that one? And pop! There goes the unhealthy focus *and* the conniption.

Notice that I didn't suggest screaming at her, telling her she was bad for wanting something potentially unsafe, or snatching the sharp object from her pudgy fingers. No. I merely suggested offering a better alternative, giving her the chance to willingly release her focus on the potentially perilous item, and redirect that focus to a better choice. I can tell you from experience, this is an awesome strategy for our grown-up selves when we begin perseverating on emotional "pointy objects," like anger and resentment. I'm not at all proposing that playing with dolls or cookie snarfing is the answer to internal discord, but choosing a better, more helpful conscious focus is. (As the Bantu proverb reminds us, "The bitter heart eats its owner.")

Here's the adult—cookie- and toy-free—version of corkscrewing yourself (or not). Say you start conjuring up how your ex-boyfriend outraged and humiliated you..."How dare he make all those promises about getting married, repeatedly telling me I was 'the only one,' and then dumping me like a hot potato when his newly divorced old girlfriend rushed back into his arms? That really sucks! I even moved to highest-crime-rate-in-the-country Camden, New Jersey, for *his* stinkin' new job! Mom warned me not to move without a solid commitment. And what about all that money he borrowed? How will I ever get it back? That scumbag! I should trash his condo. I still have a key..."

OK, you see where this is headed. You are offering yourself the emotional equivalent of an eye poke or a finger squish. Completely self-inflicted. If you are thinking right about now, *"But I'm right!"* then I ask you that brilliant question, "Would you rather be right or happy?" If we really think about it, I'll bet most of us would go for happy because wallowing in the He Dumped Me past doesn't offer us anything helpful (and it doesn't even feel good while we are in the middle of the wallow!).

In that case, the first thing to do is acknowledge that it *happened*. The whole situation may have been unpleasant, but it's over. *It's in the past.* There's nothing you can do about what *he* did, but there's everything you can do about what actions *you* elect going forward. So start distracting yourself from the negative with a list of what you gained from that relationship (presumably you didn't always consider your almost-fiancé a malodorous dirtball). You never would have snagged that awesome new finance job in Philadelphia had you not moved to nearby Camden (your hometown of Poteet, Texas, offered you very little in the way of advancement since your high-school reign as Strawberry Fest Queen). And truthfully, you've never earned this much money before, so for once in your life, it doesn't *really* matter that someone owes you $683.19. Your apartment in Philly with a fun new roommate has a great view of downtown. You can walk to work and to that nearby park with your awesome new rescue dog, Sam (your ex was allergic to dogs).

Tell yourself a new story, one in which you are not a victim but a happy, thriving success.

I'm not making light of problems, past or present; I am merely highlighting that we can make them feel much bigger or help them recede to a place where they can't harm us anymore. It all depends on the direction we fan the flame.

⌒

**Your emotions are the slaves of your thoughts,
and you are the slave to your emotions.**

—Elizabeth Gilbert

⌒

I understand that people feel the need to bemoan what's going on in their lives. Many talk shows are based on this habit of ours. *But is it helpful?* Sometimes a situation stinks, but we don't have to be thrilled about it or act like it isn't there. We *do* need to accept What Is[96] to move on. Mad happens, and if we get mad, it's our job to move that energy in the direction of what we *want* to happen, not "backward" toward the place that already caused us so much discomfort!

Phyllis Diller, that pioneering comedienne, had an effective plan for handling her ire. She said, "My recipe for dealing with anger and frustration: set the kitchen timer for twenty minutes, cry, rant, and rave, and at the sound of the bell, simmer down and go about business as usual." If I may paraphrase: Get upset if we need to, get it out, and get on with life! To upgrade her method, I suggest dispatching our frustration *consciously* and *toward* a happier goal. Why not send energy in the direction we *do* want? Because we understand that the energy we send out through our feelings helps create what we see as our "reality," incessantly reviewing an ex-boyfriend's character flaws and faux pas doesn't seem to be the strategy headed toward excellence or joy. Instead of being *anti*-ex-boyfriend, practice being *pro*-"great life for me"! We can get mad if we feel we must; we just need to make sure we give our emotions a ticket to the destination for the place we want to end up.

EXERCISE 12: The Phyllis Diller Fix 2.0

GO FOR IT!

Although Phyllis Diller did write several books, they were not overtly dedicated to emotional well-being (except that laughing seems to do wonders for our emotional health!). This trailblazing

---

96 I believe "What Is" in our life is a result of what we were thinking, how we interpreted things before. What Is does not have to be What Will Always Be, assuming that we change our minds.

comedienne is remembered more for her whacky hair and facial expressions than her psychological expertise. That said, her method of letting go of crazy can be an effective one (when tweaked just a bit). See if it works for you!

I'd like to point out that this exercise does *not* suggest we yank the person we're mad at into the room with us while we are still boiling. I've done that before, and my anger's big-muscled bouncers booted Love so far off the premises that nothing like bliss could sneak back in for anyone involved. It's *after* I deflate my anger, and do whatever I need to do to climb up toward centeredness, that I can find a way to be helpful (to myself and others). Often, just by "letting it all out" by myself, I find that's enough to remove my self-assembled barriers to peace.

1. Grab that timer again. Set it for five or so minutes, depending on where you stand with regard to your rage-o-meter.
2. Dig in to your feelings...but don't let them control you (being controlled by our emotions is not necessary or even helpful). Be very clear about the messages you are strengthening for yourself. OK, so you didn't like being treated in a disloyal way. Now tell yourself what you *do* want! "I prefer to be treated like a queen (or a rock star, or my favorite aunt whom everyone adores)!" "I prefer commitment!" "I love being appreciated! I *am* lovable!" "I am really ready for joy now!" "I *am* awesome!" Use whatever words you need to get out the frustration and deliver yourself to a better spot. *Instead of hardening what you don't want, write in the fresh, wet cement of your new path exactly what you do want!* See how this is healthier for *you* than just rerunning the "how I got duped video" in your brain? This focus takes everyone else out of your equation for your happiness. Even more, it takes you out of Victimville and back

into your own power to choose your feelings (only *you* are in charge of those, perceived "dirtbags" notwithstanding).

3. When the timer alerts you that your mad minutes have gone by, *thank yourself* for spending that time to get all those emotions out of your body.

4. Now ask yourself this famous Byron Katie question about the anger you started out with: "Is it true?" By deflating the anger, you may very well have been able to conclude that what you thought was making you so mad in the first place no longer even seems real to you!

5. Now go on with a happier day. If you find you aren't done, set the timer again, and perhaps try a different exercise.

If hollering isn't your best approach to bad-mood liberation, you can always practice breathing through your anger. I find breathing works so much better for me these days, but that wasn't always the case. Though this method isn't specifically anger-release-focused like the Phyllis Diller Fix 2.0, it is a wonderful way to relieve uncomfortable feelings. Sitting quietly and breathing through a feeling allows you to acknowledge that it is there without dissing it and also without letting it smolder, possibly allowing it to spread into a ten-alarm fire! *Recognizing anger (or any emotional discomfort), and learning how to release it, keeps it from morphing into something more.* Here's how yoga students do it:

EXERCISE 13: Three-Part Breath

GO FOR IT!

This exercise is taken right out of my best yoga classes. Conscious breathing is a key tenet of yoga, and if you already practice it, you know why. If not, this is an awesome beginner breathing exercise to help calm your nerves by placing you right in the moment (which is really the only place there is!).

1. You can do this exercise while sitting cross-legged, or lie flat as a way to really feel how the air is flowing through you. Close your eyes and exhale any stress from your face and body. Set the intention that you are going to free the uncomfortable feelings about a past situation—and free yourself along the way!
2. First, just watch your breath going in and out a few rounds. Just watch.
3. Now breathe in through your nose, and as you do, fill your belly like a balloon with the fresh air you just gifted yourself with. (I find that putting one hand on my belly/diaphragm helps me focus.)
4. Time to exhale. Really let it all out through your nose, and pull your belly button back toward your spine. As you exhale, release your negative feelings. Just let them go. Imagine them evaporating into nothingness as they leave your body.
5. Breathe in, breathe out, fully and evenly, about five or six times (or twenty, if that feels good to you!).
6. Now on to the next level: Fill your belly again, and this time, breathe in even more fresh air so that your lungs fill up enough to expand your rib cage.
7. When you let that air out, release the air from your lungs first, "knitting" your ribs back together on the exhale. Now release your balloon belly. Repeat this series five or six times as well. Attempt to keep the in and out breaths equal to each other.
8. Finally, breathing in, fill your belly and rib cage and, sipping just a bit more air, the area up to your collarbone. As you release this bigger serving of fresh air, start from the top, ending with your belly.

9. Repeat and relax! After you've done this a few times, it will seem less mechanical, and you won't have to think about the process anymore. When you are done, you will feel lighter and calmer...ahhhhh.

By "radically accepting"—breathing through—what is going on in our lives rather than stuffing it, adding fuel to it, or plugging our ears and loudly singing "La la la," we will avoid creating a monumental barrier that we'll inevitably have to climb over (and likely trip over) later. This is key to reducing suffering. What we call "pain" happens. But *suffering is what happens when we schlep pain around with us and foster it. It is our choice to acknowledge the pain and release the suffering.* I've found nonschlepping to be a pretty helpful strategy because an increase in suffering has never, not-once, produced a happier day for me.

I'm not trying to play psychologist here, I'm just offering another reminder that the way we *feel* about, or interpret, the world ends up being the way we experience it. We help ourselves immensely if we "repent" our anger because harboring bad feelings just narrows our possibilities for joy.

If we aren't at a stage in our serenity to *not* notice the "wrongs" that have been tossed our way, we would serve ourselves well to at least learn how to set them down safely. By learning to deal with anger and unbuckling it from our way of being—not forcibly prying or overtly ignoring it—we have a much easier time getting to the real purpose of this chapter (and a main goal for our life, as far as I can tell): *forgiveness.*

Before we go on, let me make plain that I'm not talking about "forgiveness" in the usual sense. Standard modern forgiveness sounds a lot like this: "Someone else did something wrong, so fabulous, magnanimous *moi*, in all my wisdom and benevolence, will deign to acquit him of his misdeed.

(And aren't I awesome for doing that?)" Or something along those lines. In any case, true forgiveness is actually nothing like that. Forgiveness is more about recognizing that whatever doesn't look like Love is just fiction anyway, so why foam at the mouth over it, deepening our own pain?[97]

About now in this kind of discussion, people tend to bring up Hitler, the poster boy for incalculable hideousness. "But it's not fiction, Kelly! Hitler was the devil! I can't forgive that!" *Of course*, what Hitler did was atrocious![98] That is not my point. My point is that by stoking the hate that he (or anyone like him) engendered, we only continue to block Love from our lives. Haven't Hitler's wrongdoings wrested enough peace from our entangledness? I fail to see how promoting more hatred and fear helps remediate what he plopped on the planet in the first place. If we keep spreading hate and fear, his heinous legacy only continues. How on earth is that helpful? Mahatma Gandhi reminded us that "anger and intolerance are enemies of correct understanding." Forgiveness *is* correct understanding, and it illustrates that we are better at Love than blame, and what a fabulous, incredibly valuable skill set that is!

The truly stunning Eva Mozes Kor, a survivor of Auschwitz and of the infamous Dr. Mengele, very factually informs us that "Forgiveness is nothing more and nothing less than an act of self-healing." Thank you, Eva!

In most cases, we aren't called upon to find the magnitude of forgiveness Hitler and his henchmen offered the world. Phew! Yet a lot of us seem unable to forgive—and therefore free ourselves from—far "lesser sins." For example, did your father (who died three years ago in May) belt-smack you every time he was drunk (which happened to be every day) until you

---

97 You may not agree that anything other than Love is fiction, but even if you don't, it is still the case that real forgiveness remains an effective way to limit our own agony.

98 And let me just confirm, his actions were dark beyond description. It is not my intent to rile us up about Hitler here. I only bring him up because he seems to represent evil incarnate. What I'll discuss in other books is that anything that doesn't look like Love isn't real, and there's a huge difference between the action and the person.

ran away at sixteen, finally escaping his incomprehensible brutality? And now that you are forty-three, do you constantly relive how mean he was, remembering the physical sting of his belt and the emotional burn of his cruelty? Do your neighbors know all about it? Does the check-out lady at the grocery store know? It truly must have been a rough experience when it was happening, but—and I don't mean to be rude or unsympathetic here—by this point, it's only *in* your head *in* the past. It's over. At 9:37 tomorrow morning, your formerly drunk, now-deceased dad is not going to show up in your living room with his pant-cinching whip, except, of course, if *you* bring him (and all those really yucky feelings) into your thoughts.

It's the same situation when it comes to renewing hatred for Hitler. Muddling around in past negativity does not serve us. It does not move us upward. Eva Mozes Kor was right: forgiveness isn't about exonerating someone for his cruelty; it's about *healing one's self*!

Attitudinally, how do we ensure that past garbage doesn't become our constant chaperone, keeping us angry and insisting that we miss out on joy? We practice looking beyond the garbage to the Love that is (temporarily) obscured by our current perspective and start telling that new, more accurate story.

For me, one of the most influential and beautiful demonstrators of this is the compassionate and funny Father Gregory Boyle. His whole life is devoted to seeing beyond the illusion of "bad" right to the heart of goodness. Father Boyle talks about "unconditional love and absolute acceptance of people." Bingo! Along the way, he helps change many other perspectives, too. The most overt way he looks past the false stuff into Love is through his work with ex-gang members in Los Angeles. In 1988, Father Boyle created Homeboy Industries "to help former gang members redirect their lives and become contributing members of their families and our community." That goal, combined with his commitment to Love, has created a group of enterprises that includes a bakery, café, catering business, merchandise sales business, and silk-screen shop. Under his umbrella of compassion are also tattoo removal; legal, health, and employment services; and various education options. Homeboy Industries is, impressively, the largest gang-intervention program in the United States and probably in the world. Through intervening with Love, Father Boyle has helped thousands of people find their beautiful truth: seeing it in them first (even when they could not) and helping them remember (even when they forgot).

From what I've read about and seen in the media, gang members seem pretty familiar with the concept of rage. Yet, when offered another version of life possibilities, a former criminal can transform who he *believed* he was back into his original self—someone who lives much more in the truth of Love than the falseness of anger.

⌒

Fear binds the world.
Forgiveness sets it free.

—*A Course in Miracles*,
W-332.1:1

⌒

In his outstanding book *Tattoos on the Heart: The Power of Boundless Compassion*,[99] Father Boyle shares poignant stories of what happens when people are offered support over censure. Through Homeboy Industries, he has helped people rewrite their stories. Now, instead of living angry and pain-filled lives created by their circumstances, expectations, or in response to how other people perceived them ("You're nothing," "You are

---

99 I highly recommend it: you will laugh, cry, and be inspired to the core.

just a troublemaker," "You won't ever get a good job with a prison record"), these former gang members see themselves as people with goodness—and good work—to offer the world. And so they do.

You don't have to be an ex-convict, a former gang member, or necessarily live in LA to rewrite your own story, one in which anger—and even just a bit of daily resentment—need not reside. You can, as with all the other forms of "repenting," start right here, right now as a plain old never-been-to-jail waiter, librarian, or surgeon. Shoot, you don't even need a tattoo.

When I bring up "rewriting" our stories, I'm not just talking about the blah-blah-blah *words* of the story. Words are OK information disseminators, as far as they go, but alone they do not have the power to yank us from our cultural hypnosis. We must *feel* something different. I'll just say it: we want to "*feel* the Love!" I contend that the Homeboys now feel more Love than anger, and that is the key to their strength and success.

EXERCISE 14: A New Chapter

GO FOR IT!

This exercise involves writing, so get out your computer, a napkin and a pen—whatever you want, as long as it offers enough permanence to let you read what you've written for at least a week.

1. Think about a certain something that makes you mad. For this exercise, please conjure up something personal—maybe that your boss has no idea of how much awesome work you do—versus your fury over high income taxes in the United States, for example.

2. Now write down how you'd like the situation to be. Use as many adjectives as you want ("delightful," "joyful," "dreamy," and "fabulous" are a few of my personal favorites). Be sure to write in present tense, not some nebulous "when."

3. When you are finished, take a few deep breaths and read it (aloud, if possible). Put this new story in your wallet, and take it with you wherever you go.

4. Read your new story in the morning. Imagine how "fabulous" and "delightful" it is to tell that story, and smile.

5. Tell *that* story during the day to yourself, or to anyone who will listen. If you just can't tell that *exact* story yet, share the prequel. That's the one that goes something like this: "I'm so excited about how my life has changed! My job is much more interesting! I never realized how fun my coworkers are!" As you are saying these things to yourself, *feel* how great it feels. As you feel your way to a new story, you are consciously creating a new story...one that will bring you many more smiles.

6. Read your chapter at night. Feel the joy of it, and fall asleep with a smile on your face, telling your new and improved story.

Even if you don't believe that "writing a happier new chapter" for your life—using your emotions as the main ingredient—is anything other than bonkers, consider what the mere act of smiling can do. Research has repeatedly demonstrated that smiling benefits our health in impressive, measurable ways, among them: boosting our immune system, releasing endorphins (our natural pain killers), reducing depression, diminishing stress, and helping us live longer. Anger, on the other hand, has its own set of well-documented negative influences, ranging from heart disease and hypertension to migraines and insomnia.

⟨⟩

**Let us always meet each other with a smile,
for the smile is the beginning of love.**

—MOTHER TERESA

⟨⟩

Given the scientific support about the influences of anger *and* smiling, it is easy to see why I maintain that forgiveness really does help the forgiver. It truly *is* a form of self-healing. Forgiveness is not about letting anyone "off the hook" (something we seem so afraid to do!); it's about being in charge of our feelings, our lives, our stories, and our joy.

What I have found is that the more I consciously tell a story of joy, the less there is to "forgive." The more I repentantly script my autobiography of happiness, the less there is to have to "look past" because what I see is closer and closer to the truth. Think of all the peace[100] we could recoup if we just practiced true, "looking beyond" forgiveness.

⟨⟩

Forgiveness
is a treasure you can offer yourself
and the world.

⟨⟩

---

100 On a personal level and a world level.

CHAPTER 9
Grateful

i thank you God for most this amazing day:
for the leaping greenly spirits of trees
and a blue true dream of sky;
and for everything which is natural
which is infinite
which is yes

—E. E. CUMMINGS

As a parent, I have counseled my children repeatedly on the importance of "please" and "thank you."[101] Of the two, "thank you" is by far the more powerful. The "thank you" vibe is an essential ingredient for basking in a happy and meaningful life. If we pray "please," we confirm a certain neediness, a not-havingness for ourselves.[102] The energy of appreciation, however, helps "densify" our recognition of joy's presence. I'm not talking platitudes here or even just echoing Miss Manners with some old-fashioned "What do you say to the nice universe?" etiquette. It's a true fact: *our thoughts of thankfulness export themselves into the space around us and literally transform it.*

---

101 "Nagged" might be their descriptive verb.
102 But *it* is always there.

First of all, **when we are busy being thankful and welcoming, we have no mental space to focus on being miserable, feeling sorry for ourselves, or comparing ourselves to others.** Because thoughts have a way of dominoing themselves down a certain path, being even a smidge thankful can help take us in the direction of more thankfulness. And really, isn't that better than feeling upset about something for *any* amount of time?

Don't take my word for it. Try it right now. Stop reading, and take a few minutes (three, perhaps!) to come up with things that draw you into gratefulness.[103] It could be any number of things, of course, because only you know what makes your heart sing. A cup of chocolate rose tea? Your dog? Your kindergarten teacher? A thick, juicy burger and a side of fries? Whatever. Just sit for a few moments, before reading more, and *feel* the joy of reviewing the good things your daily life offers you. It actually "warms" your heart, doesn't it? You may even find you are smiling! Gratefulness is *very* powerful.

Gratitude is a "nice" habit to adopt, warming your heart and all, but the Kumbaya effect is just the beginning. Gratefulness goes wayyyyyyy beyond the momentary good feeling, offering plenty of long-term and "practical" benefits we may never have intuited. The analytic types (I am related to a few) will appreciate knowing that being grateful imparts myriad *measurable* dividends. In the past twenty or so years, in fact, studies galore have documented "attitude of gratitude" improvements in surprising areas. Here are just a few:

* Better grades
* Less jealousy
* Reduced depression

---

103 A little gratefulness clarification might come in handy right about now. When I suggest we get grateful, I'm not suggesting the relief-related gratitude that comes from not getting caught running a red light or neglecting to do homework and not getting called on.

* Better sleep (less time to fall, more time to stay)
* Improved marriages
* Increased immunity
* Decreased blood pressure
* Improved performance at work
* Better interpersonal relationships
* Happier general feelings
* Boosted energy
* Better coping abilities under stress
* Higher sense of purpose

Did you just gloss over that list, or did you stop to think how amazing it is? (If you glossed, please review it!) Even though I've spent a lot of time nurturing thankfulness in my own life, when I researched all the confirmable benefits this attitude can offer, I was stunned. That gratitude can create such impressive side effects wasn't the most shocking aspect, though. What smacked me upside the head was the fact that, despite years of rigorous study, we still barely acknowledge the power of thanks! So let's examine a bit of that incredible data about cultivating gratitude.

Jeffrey Froh, Robert Emmons, Giacomo Bono, Noel Card, and Jennifer Wilson conducted one of my favorite studies, "Gratitude and Reduced Costs of Materialism in Adolescents." They questioned more than one thousand teens (ages fourteen to nineteen) and learned that gratitude (controlling for materialism) "uniquely predicts...higher grade point average, life satisfaction, social integration and absorption, as well as lower envy and depression."[104] Do you know any teenagers? This is a darn impressive finding! GPA improvement due to thankfulness! (Think of all the money we parents could save on tutors!) Who knew? Seems sort of miraculous, don't you think?

---

104 From their report published in the *Journal of Happiness Studies*, volume 12, number 2 (2010). This was published quite a few years ago, so why don't more of us know about it?

In terms of expressing gratitude outwardly, studies also show—not all that surprisingly—that romantic relationships benefit directly, too. Research by Dr. Amie M. Gordon and her colleagues[105] found that when people feel appreciated by their partners, their partners return the gratefulness and are more "responsive to their partners' needs." They are also more committed and more likely to stay in a relationship. There's an innate "gratitude reciprocity" thing. We've all experienced it; we just don't always give our attention—or actions—to it. Imagine what would happen if we did!

The wealth of life improvements that result from filling our hearts with thanks is what I call the Gratefulness Ripple. Myriad studies assess it and call it different things, but the meaning and magnitude are hard to squish into words. What really gets measured is the "closerness" to our Source that gratefulness engenders, which, *of course*, manifests in better everything! Being in a state of gratefulness is so much more who we are than being in a state of rage or frustration. Our vibration is higher in gratefulness; we can all feel it. Everyone and everything around us can feel it, too.

ᥴͻ

You pray in your distress
and in your need;
would that you might pray
also in the fullness of your joy
and in your days of abundance.

—Khalil Gibran

ᥴͻ

105 Amie M. Gordon, Emily A. Impett, Aleksandr Kogan, Christopher Oveis, and Dacher Keltner, "To Have and to Hold: Gratitude Promotes Relationship Maintenance in Intimate Bonds," *Journal of Personality and Social Psychology*, Vol. 103, No. 2 (2012), 257–74.

Also, when it comes to talking about and describing being closer to our Source, "gratitude" seems to be grasped in a more similarly understood way than even the word "love." The idea of love is so culturally and historically overloaded with expectations, guilt, sex, responsibility, and so on, that when we try to feel for it (based on what we bring with us from the past), we can often get off track. Besides, we Americans use that word like it's a multisurface cleaner and "spray" it on everything. Somehow, the English language employs the very same sequence of letters, l-o-v-e, to describe how we feel about our high-school crush, our children, our favorite shoes, *and* our connection to the Infinite. My friend Maria tells me that her fellow Italians use the word far more sparingly—more judiciously, perhaps—than we Americans do. While Italians certainly love their mothers and their kids, they would never, for example, say they "love" their new purse. It's easy to see how our one-word-fits-most habit for "love" gets confusing. Gratitude, however, is a concept—a feeling—we can more similarly internalize.

Practicing Gratitude

Dr. Robert Emmons,[106] psychology professor and thankfulness expert, tells us that some of his most famous research has demonstrated that gratitude "regulars" are 25 percent happier and generally healthier than those who neglect conscious gratefulness. That's impressive, don't you agree? Who doesn't want more energy and improved relationships? And even if academic grades aren't a part of our lives anymore, wouldn't it be fabulous to get an A in how well we live our days? Getting to grateful seems to be an important part of that. A technique Dr. Emmons has pioneered, and wonderful Oprah Winfrey has advocated for years, is gratitude journaling.

Gratitude journaling has been widely written about, practiced, and studied (there are even gratefulness apps). The basic idea is almost "duh" simple: write down what we're thankful for on a regular basis. Researchers

---

106 He cowrote the awesome "Gratitude and Adolescents" study and has also written several books on the subject.

disagree, however: is it better to write in our gratefulness journal daily or weekly? Are the results long-term? Should we write a lot, or just a few lines? These questions popped up because not all studies have uncovered stellar results. Hmmmm, how very human of us to completely miss the mark! The point is really very straightforward: to be considered real gratefulness, we just need to *feel* it in our heart space. If that means dashing off a one-liner on our phone or detailing the glory of a sunset in three handwritten pages, only *you* know what works for *you*! Once a day? Once every three days while standing on your head? Whatever ignites the spark for you! *The bottom line is to evoke—and bask in—the feeling of gratefulness.* I could write stuff to be thankful for all day long, and if I'm not emotionally engaged, I might as well be jotting down my to-do list. One pure instance of gratitude is worth an infinity of obligatory, unhearted actions.

⌒

Attention without feeling
...is only a report.
An openness—an empathy—was necessary
if the attention was to matter.

—MARY OLIVER

⌒

EXERCISE 15: Writing Our Gratitude

GO FOR IT!

Oprah says her practice of gratitude journaling has been outrageously important in her life. As I do, she believes that by focusing thankfulness on what you already have, you'll find you attract even more to be thankful for! So why not start now? You can write in a spiral notebook, a fancy gratitude book from the bookstore, on your computer, or using an app. Like most of the specifics in this book, it's not important which style you go with. *It's not the what; it's the how. The point is to go!*

Know that anything is up for grabs in the thankfulness department. Nothing is too small or too silly. For example, today I was thankful for the macaron from my freezer that originated in Paris, the reduced skunk smell on my dog and in my house, and running into a friend while erranding. Now it's your turn.

1. Think about your day, and write down five or so things for which you feel grateful. Delight in that feeling.
2. Repeat (later today, tomorrow, next week...just repeat!).
3. Repeat.
4. Repeat.
5. Never stop! Make it a habit, and enjoy the rewards.
6. Reread what you've written from time to time, and delight in remembering all the gratitude that has brought you to where you are.

Warning: Gratitude can be habit-forming. It can really make you feel high!

Gratitude journaling is a powerful way to stay in the present. However, at times I realize that being in the present moment, filled with gratitude can be a little difficult. OK, extremely difficult, at times. *Even if something feels hard, though, we are still in charge of our feelings, and we are still in charge of how we respond.* Gratefulness is always an appropriate response.

Uh-oh, I just saw some of you roll your eyes. "Right, I should be thankful that my car was totaled?" "I should be grateful my son is fighting in a war in a country I've never even visited for people I've never met?" "I should be in gratitude that my aunt Lucinda has Alzheimer's?" I totally see your point. And I don't mean to bait and switch you here, but I will say that everything in our lives exists to help us find our way back to Love: there is a reason. It's been my experience that pulling myself down to the depths of sadness only blocks me from learning and propagates my misery. Stretching myself higher and toward the light, even in hard situations, *always* feels better for me than free-falling into darkness.

When I say "Everything happens for a reason," I do not mean that God, like Santa, has a naughty and nice list, and those on God's naughty list get cancer in a coal-like response to selfish behavior or missing church all summer. No, not at all. Every event in our lives is just a result of the way we shaped our thoughts in the past and an opportunity to help us shape our thoughts *differently* in the future. So if we are sick, finding wellness can be a path back to our true selves. If something shows up in our lives that we'd really rather not experience, we can choose to be thankful for that information, which is telling us—sometimes in a whisper, sometimes in a shriek—that something needs to change. The something to change first, of course, is our minds. We can continue to argue that life sucks, but then we'd just prove ourselves right, and what fun is that?

Besides, it isn't possible to judge Infinite Reality from our perspective. We cannot know how the culmination of energies—our own and all those around us—can blend, grow, and grace us. But if we *expect* the energies to converge in Love, we can be grateful for however things unfold. We've probably all experienced pain that at one time seemed unbearable, only to recognize the gifts that came from that experience later.

Even if you don't personally buy into the lesson-learning stuff, you would still probably agree that despair is not a preferred state for most folks. Knowing we have the option to choose a path of less pain can offer incredible freedom from prolonged suffering. You would also probably agree that there have been times in your life when you know for a true fact that your own decision is what made you take either the happier path or the more miserable path. I believe *we can choose Love and gratitude or choose Other Than. Those are our options, and in the end, there's only one option.*[107] How long it takes us to choose is completely up to us. How upset we are is not a measure of how much we care, only a measure of how much we misunderstand.

WRITE IT FORWARD

If you find yourself worried about the future, you can still remain in control of the way you think and feel through gratitude. One of my favorite gratefulness "tricks" to power up a thankfulness vibe is to write a thank-you letter *in advance* for the good stuff. It puts my focus in a state of positive expectancy, like how I set my table when I've invited guests. I have every reason to believe they will show up—I invited them and they said yes, after all—so I put out the plates, napkins, and silverware. I prepare for them because I've welcomed them. This pre-thank-you note idea is sort of like that. And it works!

I first tried this method when I wanted a certain something to happen really, really, really, really badly. It had recently occurred to me what a big pile of attachment I'd created around *not* having what I really, really, really, really wanted. My perceived lack had to do with a relationship, and I'm amazed, looking back, at how incessantly I blathered on and on about not having it, how I wished it were different (which was actually another way of saying, "I wish *that* person would behave differently!"), and so on. I built a fortress for my misery and barricaded it with wall upon wall of insistence on the terribleness of it all. It so didn't meet my expectations. I fortified those walls every time I thought of, or discussed, how much I *didn't* want what I had. Of course there was no chance for Love to eke past the airtight barriers, so vigilant was I against its arrival!

---

107 This is a main point in *A Course in Miracles*, and though it took a while to sink in for me, once I let it sink, it buoyed me in surprising ways!

When I finally realized what I was doing, however, in an effort to release some of those unhelpful vibes, I wrote a note of thanks, as if the universe had already solved the situation.[108] I read it in the morning and reread it at night, just before I went to bed. I dated it a month in advance. Every time I read that note, I'd *feel* the feelings of having the relationship already improved. Those were much better sensations than the ones I'd been creating in the notness of it all, so practicing the feelings felt really wonderful in and of itself. In a month's time, it was hard to remember that the situation had ever been as bad as I had previously perceived it. In fact, things were awesome! That was cause for celebration and even more gratefulness.

In the Book of Mark, Jesus flat-out tells us to act like we've already achieved what we've prayed for: "Therefore I say unto you, all things whatsoever ye pray and ask for, believe that ye have received them, and ye shall have them." Now, he didn't bring up the thank-you-note idea—that was a later addition—but a pre-thank-you note could be our way of demonstrating that we "believe we/ye have received." After all, who would bother writing a thank-you note for something she never got?

So go ahead, write a letter of gratitude for something you would love to show up in your life. It's actually pretty fun!

EXERCISE 16: Write Believing

GO FOR IT!

I love this exercise because it's so powerful and so simple. It feels great while you are doing it...and when you are finished, there are those delightful results to soak up!

---

108 As with pretty much every idea in this book, I am not the first person to think of it. I initially heard about writing an advance thank-you note from an unidentified man on YouTube, telling the delightful, world-improving Esther Hicks how he'd experienced so many positive results using this happy method, thanks to her insights. (And she does have a lot of great insights!)

1. Create an intentionally quiet space for yourself.
2. Using note cards you love, a favorite pen, a colored pencil and a scrap of paper, your computer, whatever (because it doesn't matter), sit your buns down and start writing about what you will soon be calling a miracle!
3. On an issue you'd be grateful to see in a different light, or one in which you'd like to see a physical or emotional change, begin writing a thank-you note for the wonderful improvement, *as if it has already taken place*. To whom you address it is up to you: yourself, angels, God, To Whom It May Concern, or your great-aunt Mathilda, who has always inspired you. Again, it doesn't matter, as long as you can get into the feeling of it.
4. Before you start the physical act of writing about the reengaged relationship you have with your twin, for example, imagine how fabulous it is, you and your brother getting along for the first time in decades. Envision laughing together like you used to when you were young. Visualize the happy smile on your mom's face to see you both in sync after all these years. Think about how full it makes your heart and what a great person he is. Now imagine telling the *new* story to everyone!
5. Don't be "unrealistically specific." It isn't helpful to write about something that deep down *you* are incapable of believing could be true. Connectedness will know if energy you send out is a forgery (just remember the undercurrent of my emotions that freaked out that treadmill). If you need a new car, but very literally, you can't imagine zipping around in a Ferrari, write a thank-you note for having your transportation needs wonderfully met. If you'd love to be a size 4 but can only think of how many times diets have failed your XXL body, skip the size details and just imagine how happy it makes you to feel so healthy every day

when you wake up.[109] Truly fathom. Remember, we invite what we expect.

6. Now start writing, and as you do, *feel* how great it feels to be living what you are writing. If you feel a sticking point, if there's something that you just can't swallow, leave it out for the time being. Put in only the things you can actually imagine feeling thankful for in your life.

7. Read the thank-you note every morning and every evening for whatever time period seems realistic *to you*. (My gestation periods for these letters seem to be getting shorter. That's due, I'm sure, to what my prefiltering brain sees as "possible.")

8. When you realize the shift, *celebrate!*

This thank-you-note process uses gratitude to pull you into a better "future." Some people are naturally grateful, and that, of course, is initially easier than any retrain-myself-to-focus-on-it thank-you note. However, even if we weren't born with an eye on all the good stuff all around us, we *can* coach ourselves to be more grateful, which will, in turn, keep offering up more to be thankful for. It's such an awesome tautology! Actively feeling grateful may be the universe's equivalent of thinking of ourselves as "lucky," and we've already seen how well that attitude works out.

Another outstanding way to invite more to be grateful for is by vocalizing the good stuff already all around us, in every moment. We started out with these ideas, and they are well worth expanding. For example, being consciously thankful to family members, or anybody with whom we have a close association, is an extremely potent way to watch Love expand. When your teenage son empties the dishwasher before school—never mind that it's his job and he's *supposed* to empty the dishwasher before school—let

---

109 I absolutely do not think body size is the ultimate predictor of for health. I do, however, believe that how we *feel* about our bodies influences how much joy and health we allow them to express.

him know how much you appreciate it. When your husband fixes the leaky bathroom sink, acknowledge it with a big hug (or whatever says "Wow, are you ever dreamy!" to him), even if—or maybe *especially* if—he's a plumber and he "should" do that kind of stuff anyway. Rumi suggests, "Wear gratitude like a cloak, and it will feed every corner of your life." So true!

Look for every reason you can to express gratitude for the people in your life, and you will know that giving and receiving are actually the same thing. There are so many different ways to show thanks. And while it seems like the thankfulness is directed at someone else, I promise, the more you practice, the more you will know that gratefulness is really about you and *your* fabulousness.[110] Your focus will expand in the direction you propel it, and won't it be fantastic to enjoy so many blessings!

To give and to receive are one in truth.

—*A Course in Miracles*,
W-PI.108.1:1

What I'm telling you is simply Human Nature 101. Just think of how we are naturally more inclined to help someone who has been grateful for our own efforts. As the studies show, marriages work like that, but the whole universe works like that! Not in a retaliatory sense, as in "If you aren't grateful, I won't be nice to you." No, it's not "personal," and it's not happening from outside your own authority. It's all about energy movement. It's letting the already-there frequency of abundant joy flow in with a "Yes, thank you!" rather than blocking it with a "No way!"

---

110 This fabulosity is inclusive, wrapping Love around everything you see from this new, higher vantage point!

When we get in the practice of thank-you-ing for the most mundane of things, we delight ourselves. This habit really helps us "repent." And for those of you for whom the energy thing doesn't "resonate" yet, it's nonetheless hard to deny that when we are constantly seeking things to feel gratitude for, we don't have the brain space to focus on the negative. Again, that, in itself, is valuable!

Beyond just saying thanks to someone, or penning a thank-you note, there are uncountable creative and fun ways to show gratitude that can be meaningful for both giver and receiver. Here are just a few:

- Write a little note, and place it where the intended person will find it. I have a funny little illustrated "notes and quotes" book that I tear a sheet from, perhaps add a small note, and tape to a bathroom mirror, add to a lunch box, or put in a wallet, depending on the recipient. (No cute little preillustrated book? Sticky notes or scratch paper work just as well!)
- Cut some flowers from your backyard, and take them to your neighbor who always seems to have that egg or a cup of tahini just when you need it.
- Tell the manager. If you receive an extra dose of good service when out at the hardware store, let the owner or manager know how thankful you are for the great treatment you just received from Betty Lou or Al.
- Include a positive comment on social media. Statistically, people are much more likely to write about their bad experiences than their good ones. If you think your veterinarian is awesome, let the world know through any number of social media options.
- Leave a big, fat, out-of-the-ordinary tip.
- Have a cold iced tea ready for your mail deliverer or lawn-mowing person on a hot day.
- Take a favorite chocolate bar to someone toward whom you feel generally grateful. It doesn't have to be in response to a specific

action: your son's patient guitar teacher, your babysitter, and the custodian at your office building might all be worthy recipients of general gratefulness.

Another way we practice gratitude in my family is with a nightly tradition I call "Gimme Five." This is perfect for those times when no pen or paper is handy for journaling. (These are not "either/or" exercises, by the way...by all means, delight in as much gratitude as possible!)

EXERCISE 17: Gimme Five

GO FOR IT!

In terms of affirming the abundance in our lives, an excellent time to focus is right before we go to sleep. Often, we rewind the day, self-chastising perceived imperfections. Or we replay incidents that upset us, or *will* upset us, or *might* upset us, or would have upset us if...In any case, that kind of self-talk doesn't seem very uplifting or helpful (nor is it sleep-inducing). This exercise is an awesome gift of listing you can do for yourself as you doze off.

I hope my kids can be in the habit of consciously looking for a happiest-possible end of their day (which will help ensure a happier tomorrow), so I have them "Gimme Five" as I wish them sweet dreams. (Well, my teen has now moved on from this together-tradition, but he assures me he goes to sleep with thoughts of gratitude.)

1. Invite your child to share five things that contributed to his joyful day. In our family, I like to ask for one of the events to be directed outward—that is, something my son did that would make it to another person's "Gimme Five" list that night.

No kids at home? No worries! Give yourself five things that called up joy during the day. At first you might feel silly, but really, reviewing the good stuff can always bring a smile…and don't forget all the benefits listed by all those studies!

2. Listen and encourage, but try not to "correct." This advice goes for leading the discussion with kids, as well as yourself!

3. Fall asleep with a smile on your face.

**There are hundreds of ways to kneel
and kiss the ground.**

—Rumi

Mealtime Thankfulness

Remember how Nancy Singleton Hachisu transformed the rice she cooked with her thankfulness vibes? Well, why not add similar energetic deliciousness to *every* bite you take? Simply start sprinkling on your meals some yummy gratefulness of your own. You don't even have to make the food to affect it. (Think about those water samples in Stuttgart.) The thankfulness doesn't have to be some rote prayer with heads bowed and hands folded together, and it doesn't only have to come before the meal—both the Jewish and Muslim religions have prayers for *after* eating.

We can express our gratitude in any way that feels happiest and most true. The majority of traditions have a form of grace. In fact, "expressing thanks for food was humankind's first act of worship," says Adrian Butash in her book *Bless This Food: Ancient and Contemporary Graces from Around the World.*[111]

In our house, we often still call on the prayer my teenage son learned in preschool. Borrowing the tune of "Frère Jacques," we hold hands and try to sing it *before* we start chewing (that doesn't always happen). Sometimes we are serious, and sometimes we sing at the top of our lungs, being as silly as possible:

> God, we thank You, God, we thank You,
> For our food and family and friends, for our food and family and friends,
> We are very thankful, we are very joyful,
> Amen, Amen.

I also love the simplicity of the Japanese form of predinner thankfulness I learned from my insightful, kind friend Colleen:[112] *itadakimasu.* It means "I humbly receive." And to go a purity notch further, Buddhists and Quakers often simply quiet their minds in gratitude, in anticipation of being fully present for the meal before them. So really, we don't have to utter a single word to express our thankfulness. It's what is happening behind the scenes that counts. As Gregg Braden says, "The feeling is the prayer." So, once again, the details (aka "the rules") don't matter.

---

111 New World Library, reprint edition, August 2013.
112 She is also the one who introduced me to my husband...talk about gratefulness!

This ritual is One.
The food is One.
We who offer the food are One.
The fire of hunger is also One.
All action is One.
We who understand this are One.

—Ancient Hindu blessing

Thankful Reciprocity

When we do something nice for someone, we usually expect a thank you or *some* acknowledgment. I am nobody to say that receiving a thoughtful note in response to some act of kindness isn't delightful. However, if a response doesn't show up, *it's important that the satisfaction of our giving be our giving.*

I'm someone who really enjoys finding the "perfect" gift. Frequently for Christmas presents, I collect my favorite things the current year has introduced me to and send them to friends and family whose distance means I haven't been able to share my discoveries in person. I admit, despite how excited *I* get about the gifts, they are not all as well-loved by others. Like the time I sent my godchildren composters. Or the holiday season I sent Sharpies, a glass pitcher, and Dr. Emoto's *Hidden Messages in Water*.[113] Six months later, while visiting one of the recipients (a very, very dear friend), we began talking about that book, and she responded, "Oh, that's what those pens were for!" Then there was the handmade rosebud

113 Recall that Dr. Emoto was the man who wrote words on bottles of water, transforming the shape of the water crystals in the "treated water."

purse I gave my glamorous sister one year, thinking it was a match to her fashion instincts...it became a white-elephant gift!

Fortunately, I don't care what friends do with the gift I give them because I have so much fun planning it, making or buying it, and even sending it! The joy is already there for me, before anyone even opens the box. That's much better for me than being dependent on anyone else's gratitude for my own happiness.

All that said, I am a big fan of writing thank-you notes to other people (not just ones to myself in the future!). I write them for my own benefit, too, because they give me a double dip, present-wise. First I receive the gift, then I get to think about how someone took time to think about me, make or purchase something specifically for me, and then ensure I receive that something special!

Not everyone appreciates a thank-you note, however, as I learned once, many, many years ago. I was in New York City, hunting for my first job out of college, and passed a man walking down the street. He stopped me in the middle of the sidewalk crowd and asked, "What are you smiling about?" I told him I was looking for a job and was excited about how nice everyone was to me.

"Really? What do you do? Most people don't walk around smiling like that when they're in the middle of a job hunt," he responded.

I have no idea what I answered because, frankly, I had no idea what I could "do." At that point, I could speak a few languages and was willing to work hard, but I couldn't even type or add numbers very well. Whatever I answered, he acted impressed, introduced himself as Sumner, and handed me his business card. Then he suggested we meet "over there" at 5:30. "Over there" happened to be the lobby bar of a big hotel. Even being fresh off the turnip truck, this seemed a bit odd to me, but, what the heck, this was New York City; I probably just didn't know the standard operating procedures yet.

So at 5:27 p.m., I found my suit-wearing self in the "over there" dark-ish lobby, awaiting the expected job interview. Sumner sat down next to me and began asking reasonable, jobish questions. Then, just a few minutes into the meeting, he stared straight at me and asked, "Now, Kelly, if I get a job for you, what will you give me?"

Well, I looked right back at him and told him the truth: "My mother always told me that when someone does something nice for you, you should always write him a thank-you note." I believe that was the end of our interview.

THE RIGHT WAY TO BE GRATEFUL

OK, so there's really not a single right way to be grateful. All these ideas for thankfulness expression are merely suggestions and reminders to be in—really *in*—whatever moment we find ourselves and to consciously look for the good that's surrounding us. *There is always good surrounding us; what we allow in depends on how wide we open our hearts.*

CHAPTER 10

Kale versus Cookie Dough

∽

The shortest interval between two points
is the awareness that they are not two.

—ERIC MICHA'EL LEVENTHAL

I'VE WAITED UNTIL I'VE HAD the chance to explain some important concepts before overtly bringing up what I've been conveying at some level in every chapter: *there's really only Love.* Any time we think we see anything else, we are forgetting our union with our Infinite Source: Love. Until now, most of us have been experts at practicing *not* remembering Love. We do this largely by judging what we see (or what we *think* we see), regretting the past, fearing the future, blaming others, and forgetting to be grateful. We are geniuses at living in every other moment but this one (even though "now" is really all there is). We act like things must be good or bad, right or wrong; that we have to feel guilty about the past; or that—to be "responsible"—we should worst-case-scenario the future! All of this only puts us out of alignment with what is true. It's what I call the Kale versus Cookie Dough duality of life.

I am quite an overachiever in the field of duality myself, having contributed to it so intensely for so long. This is not, you will see, a self-congratulatory statement. When I ran Smart Foods Healthy Kids, for example, I spent uncountable hours highlighting "healthy" and "unhealthy" things to eat. In lectures, videos, presentations, articles, and private consultations, I was *very busy* telling people that their meal and snack selections would either *improve*—in a very kaleish sort of way—their blood pressure/heart/muscles/weight/fill-in-the-blank or help *cause* cancer/diabetes/obesity/fill-in-the-malady—as in cookie dough. This was just my way of being helpful.

⌒⟶

Some Famous Opposites

Black	White
Male	Female
Either	Or
Bert	Ernie
Rich	Poor
Up	Down
In	Out
Harold	Maude
Bad	Good

⌒⟶

I was adamant. Judgy. I didn't yell, of course, while expounding my opinions—I have a high voice, and I'm a big smiler—but my message was intransigent. I mean, I'd *really* studied all the studies, and they said...but wait! Every month, research was published that would contradict the previous study or, worse, impugn longstanding common sense (Butter? Meat? Caffeine? Wine? Eggs? And yes, even *kale*?). With not a little irony, the definitions of healthy and unhealthy still seem to change regularly, according to which interest group, corporation, or movie star has just found/decided on the "better" option. And, wow, do people get healthier-than-thou on each other. (I should know—I have!) Anyone with a heartbeat could feel all the duality of *right versus wrong* that my well-meaning healthiness comrades and I have piled up over the years (though "duality" may not be everyone's identifying code name). No wonder that business was seldom fun.

So get on with it, Kelly—clear up this "duality" stuff and what it has to do with sugary food and green leafy vegetables.

Well, it's such a big concept to chew on, I thought food would be a helpful way to serve it. Duality in the spiritual sense is basically the Kale versus Cookie Dough of our struggle to remember our connection (aka our truth, natural bliss, or any number of names for *it*). I say "struggle" because we have this crazy-making tendency to pit everything against what we perceive as its opposite (like kale or cookie dough). Or, at the very least, we judge something as positive or negative (like kale or cookie dough). Duality is the idea that one thing can be bad, while something *else* can be good (pick any pair of opposites). *I'd say duality is the opposite of unity, except in unity, there is no "something else," no opposite.*

Why care? For one thing, all that labeling and judging is exactly what keeps us from our joy in the moment. Not to get too woo-woo here, but duality isolates us from our "Is-ness" because we are so focused on what Isn't! Many philosophies compare what we call "real life" to a dream. When we aren't "dreaming," we can remember the unity of our truth, which is where we all started out, way back at the beginning. Back when we still felt connected to our Source. Before we forgot that we were one with Source, and started to believe that everything is separate and defined by being separate. Before we fell asleep.[114]

---

114 In the Bible, we are told that Adam fell asleep, but did you ever see the verse where he woke up? No, not yet. There's also the Buddhist story in which someone asks the Buddha if he's some kind of god, angel, or otherworldly being. "No," he says simply, "I'm awake."

Uh-oh. Even if you agree that we were created in Love, you may not be buying into the dream thing, or this unity-of-Love/truth-of-who-we-are stuff. I can hear some of you now, insisting again that things in life *are bad!* Things in life *are good!* How could we live our lives if we didn't label things? I know, this may be challenging to interpret, but let's crank open a window in our brains for a minute and release a few of our musty, old assumptions to make room for new ideas. You know, *repent.* Earlier in this book, we noticed holes in some very basic premises on which we build our lives—stuff is solid, time is "real," we don't "see" everything we think we see—those kind of details. **Our beliefs about what we "see" are only "true" or "real" based on our limited focus and our individual interpretations of the past.** Yet somehow, we've Velcroed, super-glued, *and* padlocked our personal and cultural conceptions of right and wrong, good and bad to those potentially false ideas. At least until something righter or wronger comes along. (So eggs are *good* now, are they?)

There's a detail in the title sequence of *Downton Abbey* that caused me to consider just how ridiculous we humans can be about what we claim is important, right, valuable, or in some way A-OK. In a mere blip, just after a close-up of a copper cooking pot, is a scene of a someone setting a fancy table. There is a hand measuring—with a ruler—the distance of the cutlery from the plate. The first time I noticed it, I chuckled and thought, "Oh, isn't that silly! The things people used to think were so important... like the distance between knives and plates actually matters!" But then it hit me: why is meticulously measuring the span of silverware any different than much "etiquette" and rules we keep (and foster judgments with) these days? Why *do* ladies still, frequently, go first? Why *can't* we put our elbows on the dinner table? Why is it disrespectful to keep a hat on when a flag passes?[115]

---

115 And in the not-so-distant past there were these social rules: wearing a high-collared long dress to the beach, hiding a woman's ankles in public, and never hugging a royal.

The world was my oyster
but I used the wrong fork.

—Oscar Wilde

I don't advocate dumping certain conventions that make sense for us now. For example, I wouldn't mind the teensiest bit if my youngest son would always chew with his mouth closed. There are obvious and immediate benefits to following *some* prescripts! I'm merely highlighting that more than a few of our cultural norms don't actually serve us anymore—if they ever did—yet not following them would at least attract social censure...and certainly inhibit our popularity!

Through so many sources, we are actively encouraged to align to protocols that someone, or group of official someones, deemed necessary to our happiness, success, or acceptability.

I'm not dissing politeness here. What I am suggesting is that blindly following "rules" might actually cost us *a lot*—a reunion with our true selves, for example. If we unthinkingly continue to bind ourselves to cultural ideas instead of opening our hearts and minds to possibilities beyond what we know or have imagined,[116] we'll delay the happiness that is waiting for us *right now*. I know plenty of people keeping themselves quite busy doing the "right things," wearing the "right clothes," and eating the "right foods," and not feeling very happy about any of it.

---

116 That miracles are perfectly normal, for instance, or that being filled with joy is not even hard!

⟪ ⟫

The criterion of what is possible in any age is derived from
that age's rationalistic assumptions. There are no
"absolute" natural laws to whose authority
one can appeal in support of one's prejudices.

—CARL JUNG

⟪ ⟫

I am infinitely thankful that many people throughout history were brave enough to rethink some of the accepted peculiarities of their time. I can't imagine not being able to vote or having to live in a society in which slavery was overtly accepted.[117] Thank you, Abraham Lincoln! Thank you, Mahatma Gandhi! Thank you, Martin Luther King! Thank you, Harvey Milk! Thank you, John Muir! Thank you, Susan B. Anthony! Thank you, Mother Teresa! Thanks to all those leaders who were able to think beyond the separating habits of social propriety and help us move toward our more connected state of being!

My major beef with all the man-made rules is just that: they are man-made and temporal, yet we—consciously and unconsciously—constrain our lives as if they were true. They keep us in two-ness. All our rights and wrongs, our goods and bads, and our acceptables and prohibiteds fuse us to duality.

Which naturally brings me back to food.

I assume that, by now, you've heard about the obesity and diabetes epidemic in the United States. According to the last stat I saw, we Americans

---

117 We still have many opportunities for improvement, but we are headed in the right direction.

top the list of this planet's large folks. The citizens of France, however, did not even make the top ten, despite the fact that they are known for their rich (and delicious!) foods.

Why is that? My bets are on our kale-versus-cookie-dough adamancy: *orthorexia nervosa.*[118]

⟨⁓⟩

Orthorexia Nervosa:
fixation on righteous eating.

⟨⁓⟩

University of Pennsylvania psychologist Paul Rozin[119] has investigated our attitudes about "good" foods and "bad" foods and has demonstrated the beliefs around good and bad to be quite culturally variable. There is no "absolute" thumbs-up or thumbs-down when it comes to how we nourish ourselves. (Really? Because the last study I saw said...)

The articulate Michael Pollan, in his beautifully-written book *In Defense of Food: An Eater's Manifesto*, writes poignantly about Rozin's findings. The topic, innocently enough, is Americans' views on eating chocolate cake. Pollan explains that, "'Guilt' was the top response. If that strikes you as unexceptional, consider the response of French eaters to the same prompt: 'celebration.'"[120]

---

118 I am not unaware of choices made due to costs of eating fresh vegetables over, say, highly subsidized, processed foodstuff. What I'm talking about here has to do with the energy we create around food choices.

119 Dr. Rozin comes up with some fascinating insights! More recently than his survey referencing chocolate cake, he wrote about the cultural evolution of "disgust." He's an awesome rethinker.

120 This reference comes from page 79 of *In Defense of Food: An Eater's Manifesto*, but I also like Mr. Pollan's summary from that same book: "Eat food. Not too much. Mostly plants." That is a wonderfully nondualistic way to talk about food! (Everything I've read by this man has been well worth reading. He always makes me think/rethink!)

What? Not a hint of self-loathing? Don't the French care about fat grams? Aren't they worried about their cholesterol levels? What would that piece of chocolate cake do to their glycemic index? Is the cake organic? Is the chocolate free trade? How long would a slice take to work off on the elliptical?

Could it be that we Americans have piled up such a heap of rights and wrongs about food that we can no longer enjoy the simple pleasure of eating? Does anything like cake have a chance of entering our preprogrammed digestive prejudices and *not* turning into some form of manifested guilt? Is it possible that the negative messages we send our cells affect our ability to process food in a Love-filled manner?

We don't find truth by *fighting* false: we find truth by simply not noticing anything else.

Sit down if you aren't already because I'm about to propose something most food Nazis may not appreciate. (I say this as a former food Nazi.) *What if we gratefully ate what made us feel good and just didn't eat what didn't make us feel good, without making a big to-do about it?* What if we listened to our bodies instead of outside "experts" and truly enjoyed every morsel we popped in our mouths? I'll bet cake *and* every green veggie in the world would all seem more celebratable, unadulterated by judgment and duality.

My husband—fond of neither kale nor cookie dough—sure loves a good pepperoni pizza. When pressed to philosophize, he will heartily assert that pepperoni pizza really *is* the secret to life (along with, perhaps, red wine and pretzels). He claims that by the time he is interviewed for still coaching lacrosse and robotics at 160 years of age, the scientific community will have to accede to his pepperoni pizza wisdom. In terms of food and health, it's hard to argue with someone who is almost never sick (unless, he will tell you, he is emotionally upset about something) and, though he doesn't work out much, is in shockingly good shape. As far as healthiness goes, he's a natural nonduality genius!

My brilliant friend Jeremy is an even more extreme testament to how our ideas about what we "consume" can prime outcomes that respond to those very beliefs. Though he is a well-respected medical doctor with a background that includes Harvard and Columbia Universities, he often eats glass and fire (not simultaneously, though I don't know what he'll come up with next). The first time I witnessed the Shock Doc's unusual swallowing skills, I marveled, "Wow, how can Jeremy eat broken light bulbs and flaming torches with no problem, and I can't even have a piece of pizza without suffering?"[121] Sure, Jeremy trained his abilities, but isn't that exactly what we all do at some level, consciously or unconsciously through our expectations and assumptions? Do I see fire eating as dangerous (ummmm, *yes*), and does Jeremy just see it as entertaining?[122]

What I'm highlighting here is that our beliefs about *what* we ingest have a huge impact on *how* we digest them. If we tell our bodies what we are eating is chocolate cakeishly, guiltily "bad" for us, how can we expect our cells to deny the commands they are receiving? And science has now shown us that we can no longer blame our genetic makeup for 100 percent of what happens to us, either.

---

121 As a baby, I was diagnosed with celiac disease. I no longer have wheat issues, which, again, is a story for another bottle of wine, or cup of tea, if you prefer…

122 He can also do fabulous magic tricks and read the serial numbers from dollar bills in another room. His belief system seems to offer him more fun than most of our belief systems offer us!

The enthusiastic and joy-filled Dr. Bruce Lipton can back me up on this one. He has shed a great deal of light on "epigenetics," a compelling new branch of genetics. "Epi" means "above," so epigenetics is translated as "above the genes." This science demonstrates that we are not deterministically tied to our genetic inheritance, as was once believed. The expression of genes can be greatly influenced from the "outside"; perhaps even by negative feelings and concepts about what we are eating. In his excellent book *The Biology of Belief: Unleashing the Power of Consciousness, Matter, and Miracles*, Dr. Lipton elegantly highlights how, essentially, Heisenberg's Observer Effect takes place in our cells, and we are the observers! *Even on the cellular level, we invite what we expect.*

We perceive the environment and adjust our biology, but not all of our perceptions are accurate. If we are
laboring under misperceptions, then those misperceptions provide for a misadjustment of our biology.

—Bruce Lipton, PhD

This idea is illustrated powerfully by one of the early adaptors in the New Age. Ram Dass, born Richard Alpert, is a beautiful spiritual leader whose path included Stanford, Harvard, LSD, and India. Harvard wasn't so crazy about the LSD part and fired him, which left him more time for the LSD and India parts. In India he found his guru, Neem Karoli Baba (also called Maharajii) about whom Ram Dass tells a fascinating story in the documentary *Fierce Grace*. Maharajii asked Ram Dass if he could try some of his LSD. So Ram Dass did what any good disciple would do: he honored the request of his teacher. Offering the hallucinogens, however, worried Ram Dass. Really, who wants to give your guru a bad trip? Or worse, kill him? Talk about bad karma! So he provided Maharajii a choice of several different pills, holding them in his open palm for selection. Much to the pupil's horror, instead of selecting *one*, the guru scooped each and every pill from Ram Dass's hand and popped them *all* in his mouth. The student was aghast. *The guru was unaffected.* Maharajii had no belief that the LSD was real—experts would tell us he was in a state of nonduality—so anything that wasn't Love had no power to affect him.

I have no current inclination to partake of fire, glass, or LSD, but I sure would love to retrain myself to interpret everything I eat as neither "good" nor "bad"; just nondual. I'm closer than I was—thanks to an exceedingly low bar—but it's safe to say I'm not there yet. My kids, ever-vigilant to my spiritual progress, pointed out recently that I cannot accurately call myself "label-free," still largely preferring organic and the not-so-processed over their opposites.[123] I suppose the day I nonchalantly stock our pantry with "Dinamita Doritos" is the day I will have reached the ultimate state of nonduality. Until then, my boys loudly lament their red, crunchy absence.

However, in an absolutely wild departure from who I was when I ran Smart Foods Healthy Kids, I *have* adapted a delicious cookie dough recipe, which I would like to share here (if you knew me in my food Nazi days, you'd be *shocked* at this). I roll the dough into balls that I put in the freezer so we can enjoy cookie dough at any time![124] For those who prefer actual from-the-oven cookies, this dough turns into treats that are soft, thick, and irresistible.

---

123 See what I mean? If I were totally nondual, I would see no "opposites." For now I'm thankful for "duality lite."

124 For those of you concerned about raw eggs, just add a little liquid—like milk—instead of eggs if you don't plan on ever baking the dough. Or just add salmonella to the list of things to not be in duality about.

EXERCISE 18: Make Scrumptious and Love-Filled Cookie Dough
(or Soft, Scrumptious, and Love-Filled Cookies)

GO FOR IT!

Ingredients:

1½ c. butter, melted (3 sticks)
1½ c. brown sugar, gently packed
¼ c. granulated sugar
1/3 c. honey
4½ t. vanilla

4½ c. flour
2 t. baking soda
1 T. cornstarch
¾ t. salt
1½ t. ground cinnamon

2 egg yolks, room temperature, slightly beaten
2 c. chocolate chips (I like dark chocolate chunks.)

Directions:

1. Set out all the ingredients on your counter, and practice a little gratitude. How awesome to be able to have all these things at your fingertips! How wonderful that the dedication of so many different people you don't even know is helping make these cookies possible: the wheat farmer, the dairy farmer, the cows, the chickens, and the like.

Your friends and family are going to be so happy when they bite into these! (See how we really are all connected?)

2. Now gently melt the butter on the stove in a medium-size pot. When melted, add sugars and stir until blended. Now add honey and vanilla, and set aside to cool. Doesn't it smell good already?

3. Place all dry ingredients in a large bowl and stir with a whisk. (I like to put my baking soda and cornstarch through a little strainer, just to get out any clumps.)

4. Add the eggs to the cooled butter mixture, blend, and add this mixture to the dry mixture. Blend by hand with a wooden spoon, all the while imagining how lucky you are to be making cookies and how delicious they are going to taste! The cookies can serve as your own Dr. Tiller–like IIED Device!

5. Fold in the chocolate chips, enjoying a few along the way.

6. Refrigerate the dough for a couple hours (or more).

7. Now you can either eat the yummy dough or bake delicious cookies. If you opt for baking, just heat the oven to 325°F, and while it's heating, form large blobs of dough. Place them on a parchment-paper-covered cookie sheet. Bake for about 11 minutes, and remove (they won't look quite done).

8. Leave them on the cookie sheet for a few minutes—or as long as you are able to resist—sending them each a little thankfulness, and then enjoy them, share them, and delight in how awesome you are!

9. I have absolutely no idea how many they make or how long they last. What I don't eat or bake (because my husband, oddly, doesn't appreciate cookie dough, I bake some for him), I put in the freezer, in little balls.

Through all this foodishness, I hope to help the idea of nonduality become an everyday, feel-it-in-the-bones concept. I've tried for years to understand nondualism as it is explained by mystics, philosophers, and teachers, and it was a hard nut for me to crack. As you know from the exercises in this book, however, when we feel things happening in our bodies, we tend to find them more "believable." The necessity to eat for survival ensures that we can all (theoretically!) practice nonduality through our dietary attitude. We each have the opportunity to realize that *our beliefs about food—guilt versus celebration—may simply be unexamined faithfulness to the past*, or the news, or even advertising![125]

WOULD YOU RATHER?

My youngest son and I love to play that stimulating game "Would You Rather...?" While it is not explicitly about food, we often bring food into it, finding so much to be enthusiastically repulsed by when it comes to the possibilities of consumption! We consider the game hilarious (though my husband and oldest son deem our entertainment exceedingly disgusting). This form of frequently distasteful fun traditionally involves contraposing one gross option against a theoretically equally gross option, choosing a "rather," and explaining why.

One fourth-grader with excellent Would You Rather...? skills posed this impressive question: "Would you rather have a *baby* out of your very own *stomach* (much shuddering and facial revulsion accompanied this part of the query) or...eat your dog?"[126] Our favorite WYR question, though, is

---

125 Let me set straight, however, that we must be grounded enough in our new beliefs (and energetic acknowledgements) to change our bodily responses to perceived dangers or allergens. I do not recommend that you run out and gulp a handful of LSD, suck on a lighted torch, or even nibble on a croissant if you have wheat issues.
126 Rest assured, "having a baby" has been the overwhelming "rather" on that one, though I did find it ironic that the *best* thing that ever happened to me was one of the worst things this young boy could imagine!

this one, gleaned from the Internet: "Would you rather sweat mayonnaise or poop a softball?" OK, it *is* gross, but can't you see why we laugh?

Having worn thin the gross factor, we have mostly transformed the nature of our questions from "icky" to "delightful." Now our subjects more frequently go along these lines: Would you rather have a permanently filled, twenty-flavor ice-cream maker in the house or enjoy snickerdoodles with every meal (including breakfast)? And, because superheroes are the *most* interesting topic in the universe, "Would you rather have x-ray vision or be able to fly at the speed of light?"

We find these comparisons more agreeable to consider than the gross-out options. My husband, however, still resists our Would You Rather...? game on philosophical grounds that go beyond poor taste. He feels any game with just two choices is too limiting to be worthwhile. Why settle for "either/or"? he wonders. Why choose from just two options when the world has so many, many possibilities?

I agree with him about the ridiculousness of only two options,[127] but I actually believe most of us on this planet play WYR all the time with our own life decisions. Work hard *or* have fun? Be rich and famous *or* a poor nobody? Be good at math *or* excel in the arts? The majority of us act like one choice automatically precludes the other. As if all the stuff we generally label one way must necessarily have an opposite!

But *why?*

What if there were no edges, or opposites, or anything "other"? What if all we really looked at and saw was pure, sweet, joy-filled Love?

---

127 Not enough to stop playing WYR, but I *do* understand his point.

EXERCISE 19: Edgy

GO FOR IT!

Now that you have likely released some ideas that may have limited you before, and you've had a bit of practice going beyond your immediate senses, this should be an especially interesting exercise.

1. With your eyes closed, start out by contracting every muscle in your body. In doing this, you can really feel the chair or floor that's supporting you. Stay squished and restricted for several seconds.

2. Now let go, and as usual, find the quiet in your heart space. Breathe in and out a few times. Follow your breath. We've been breathing through our noses and lungs, so now try to imagine the air coming in and out of *all* of you, as if there were no body separate from Everything Else. Kind of like a sponge breathing from every pore.

3. With your eyes still closed, go to the "edge" of where you think your body is. Notice how it's not so easy to feel the chair anymore. Go out in every direction—360 degrees—to find the edge. Remember to breathe.

4. Keep going. Intend yourself out and out and out. Imagine there is no boundary to your body. Close your eyes and breathe, and this time, breathe through and *out*—out your cells, out your body, out to the universe. What you will find is that there is no "edge." There is no hard stop to your consciousness. It truly is infinite. There is no "other."

5. Don't worry if you found an edge today. Your intention will take you farther and farther out each time you practice this expansive exercise. And you will feel better and more relaxed by just practicing!

I completely understand the upsetting-ness of things not being good or bad, of things not having edges that separate. *Our lens has been so focused on either/or that a new perspective can feel like we've put our shoes on the wrong feet.* When I first began investigating Buddhism, for example, and came upon the concept of "nonattachment," it absolutely undid me. "But I *love* my family! I *love* my friends! I would never want to be detached from them!" I had mistakenly interpreted nonattachment to mean *detachment*, as in "not caring." But nonattachment is really about not clinging to an expected outcome and then basing our happiness on that outcome. Nonattachment doesn't "rather" us into duality. No wonder Buddhism is called "the Middle Way."

Of course, Buddhism isn't the only philosophical proponent of middleness. Aristotle referred to his idea of balance as the Golden Mean. The *Qur'an* speaks of the middle way to "bear witness to the truth before all mankind." Confucius taught the "Doctrine of the Mean." And even in our own current vernacular—despite its apparent elusiveness—we commonly reference that "happy medium." Whatever words we use, it is certain that finding ourselves balanced in the middle, rather than teetering judgmentally on the extremes, is a far more comfortable—and divinely accurate—way of being in the world. Ahhhhhhhh...[128]

Stop Feet

When I was a new mom, I attended a mother-child preschool class taught by a wise and gentle woman named Mary. She offered practical advice—napping, biting, pooping, and so on—and insights that went far beyond parental stratagems. I benefited immensely from all she so kindly shared. A lesson that greatly informs me still is "Stop Feet." It turns out, it is much more helpful, when we see our toddler darting toward an oncoming Mac truck, to yell, "Stop feet!" than "Don't run!" Teacher Mary explained that

---

128 I am not detached from all outcomes yet, but I worry much less frequently than I used to, and I don't scream back at politicians on TV anymore.

in telling our children not to run, what their brains hear is that last emphasis: *"Run!"* What a great lesson for life! **We can know what we don't want, but unless we articulate what we do want, how can we create the yes?** A big pile of yes is so much easier to hatch into awesomeness than a big pile of no!

Of course, most parents theoretically grasp that it is more effective to inform our kids what we *want* them to do than what we do *not* want them to do. With that, we change the focus, and we change the direction everyone tends to look. The logic is inescapable and brilliantly simple. Yet we adults show surprisingly anemic aptitude in the Stop Feet Department. (Or, maybe it's just me.) Mostly we tell our kids, ourselves, the world: "Don't run!" We use different words, of course. Our grown-up version of "Don't run!" shows up as the other don'ts we cascade through our conversations with life:

* Don't leave the lid up.
* Don't forget to call me!
* Don't leave me!
* Don't hit your brother.
* Don't talk to me that way.
* Don't think of elephants.[129]

The "don't" spotlight makes it harder to see what's outside the defined circle of focus. It is not the middle way.

Besides the variations of "Don't run," so many other dualistic sayings pepper our language without our even noticing them. We've heard them for so long, we may never have even thought about them! But by unwittingly investing in them, we find the dividends of what we do *not* want. They *prime* us. And they show up in all sorts of sentence permutations that

---

129 Didn't you immediately think of elephants? Exactly!

can begin with words other than "Don't!" Perhaps you've heard yourself
say any of the following:

* No pain, no gain.
* All good things must come to an end.
* Damned if you do, damned if you don't.
* Too good to be true.
* No good deed goes unpunished.
* I'll be happy when it's over.

Sayings like these are another reason why a focus on gratitude is so
important. Let's double back to that topic for a moment. We unthinkingly
recite sayings like the ones listed (and so many more) without realizing
how much they inspire us to plan for the worst, and definitely *not* to be
thankful, or even not prejudge. They keep us deeply embedded in a dualistic way of thinking. But thankfulness, withholding judgment, remaining
neutral, and just letting things be do not divide.

MAYBE

Besides, hasn't the past shown us that we don't really know enough about
a situation to judge how it will work in our lives in the long haul? Think
about how many times you can look back in your life and be thankful for
something you once perceived as "bad." There is a famous Buddhist "parable" that explains the concept something like this:

An elderly farmer's only horse ran away one afternoon, and the
neighbors gathered around him in dismay, sympathetically articu-
lating his "really bad luck."

"Maybe," responded the farmer, with a shrug.

The following day, his horse returned with three wild-horse buddies to greatly add to the farmer's wealth. The neighbors were astounded by his good fortune and proclaimed, "How fabulous for you!"

"Maybe," repeated the farmer.

The next day, as the farmer's son was beginning to train the new horses, he was bucked from the wildest one and broke his leg. Again, those interested neighbors commented on the situation: "What terrible luck that is!"

And, once more, the farmer's reply was a simple, "Maybe."

The next day (it was a busy week in that village!), military officials showed up to conscript men into their company. Of course, a young man with a broken leg was of no use to them, so they left him behind. The neighbors, always ready to observe and comment, said, "How lucky you are that your son can't go off to battle with that badly broken limb!"

By now you know that this nondualistic farmer just looked at them and mustered, "Maybe."

At the risk of smacking the obvious in all our faces, I'll highlight that, though we may not be farmers with horse-training sons, not one of us can accurately judge "good" or "bad" in the minispans of our own life chapters. For one thing, we just don't have the spacious perspective to do that.[130] By remaining nonjudgy about what's happening to us—by not clinging to what we perceive as positive or negative (and then adding drama to it)—we can remain connected to the nondualistic Love that is the truth of the situation.

---

130 For another thing, nothing is "good" or "bad"; it just "is." Everything is about our response!

Releasing Two-ness

I know this duality stuff seems foreign at first. But, as with most opportunities to change the way we think, we start by acknowledging there *is* a different way to think! Being awake and open-minded to our oneness will open the door for our patient, nondual truth.

Chew on this:
Can we really be pro-peace and successfully
"fight" evil?
Must we make "war" on drugs,
cancer, and poverty
to help dissolve them?
Can we delight in a piece of cake?
Do we know *for certain* that something is
"good" or "bad"?

CHAPTER 11

Take Joy Seriously

Sometimes your joy is the source of your smile,
but sometimes your smile can be the source of your joy.

—THICH NHAT HANH

OF ALL THE QUESTIONS TO ask ourselves on a regular basis, one of the most important (maybe *the* most important!) is *"How much joy did I invite in today?"* My own opinion aside, happiness does seem to be quite the hot topic lately, as exhibited simultaneously by our bookshelves, best-seller lists, and our aforementioned reliance on antidepressants. Who doesn't want to be happy?[131]

But if happiness is so all-important, why, I will ask again, do we devote so little of our attention to it? And even when we do consciously attend to joy, it seems largely to be in a "seeking it out" way rather than just gently, easily letting it in. Perhaps that's because we are so darn serious about most things, culturally speaking, that we haven't considered there's a perfectly fabulous—*super easy*—alternate route to happiness. We perceive "getting

---

131 And, because words can frequently kerfunkle us, let me say that by "happy," I do not mean that short-lived spike that occurs when, say, we win $100 from a lottery ticket or find the perfect party dress. I'm using "happy" as a synonym to joy. I mean those good, peaceful feelings that keep us smiling, *even when!* Some folks argue that "joy" is less ephemeral than "happy." Let's not let semantics inhibit meaning.

down to business" as somehow more valuable than having fun or en*joy*ing ourselves. We do fun when it fits in, after the "critical" stuff. Why isn't "joy" higher on our priority list, and why do we assume it can't possibly be a legitimate factor in success?

I'm not sure where to chicken or egg this issue, so I'll start with education because most schools are such shining examples of institutionalized seriousness and define success largely through preestablished syllabus conformity. Many no longer offer those nugatory classes like music and PE. After all, what's so "essential" about singing or running? (Of course you know by now that I claim those courses are probably more "essential" than much of the core curriculum.)

The other day, for example, my son asked me how to calculate the area of a hexagon. Cute that he assumed I still possess such knowledge, but even though I once learned to measure hexagons, as he is doing through his how-to-go-to-a-good-college classes, I have passed all these subsequent decades without needing—even once—to exploit *any* six-sided-measuring knowhow. So, I ask you, how "essential" is that? On a regular basis, however, I must navigate my days as a kind and loving family member, a community contributor, and, hopefully, a not-too-lame friend. To assume each of these roles successfully, *my own foundational joy is essential.* With that in mind, I'll daringly propose, unless you have a career in stop-sign designing, that you, too, would find hexagonal measuring (and much of established memorization-based curricula) a less valuable skill than joy making. Oscar Wilde had a point when he said, "Education is an admirable thing, but it is well to remember from time to time that nothing that is worth knowing can be taught."

Of course, we initiated this country's educational system with some serious scholastic gravity. At an amazing exhibit in New York's lion-guarded public library, I once witnessed, up close and personal, the surprisingly diminutive book we Americans selected as our very first textbook. Called

The New England Primer, it was basically the foundation of most New World academic curricula prior to the 1790s. It didn't exactly foster an attitude of lightness and hilarity. If you were sitting in a classroom with other colonial kids, you would memorize your ABCs with the aid of these delightful and inspiring didactic ditties:

A   In Adam's Fall
     We sinned all.

F   The idle Fool
     is whipt at school.

Y   Youth's forward slips
     Death soonest nips.[132]

Well, now that we all know about priming, can it be any surprise that just a few years later (relative to human history), we've dropped art classes from the schedule? We wouldn't want artsy idleness to give way to whipping. And because death, according to the letter Y, comes so soon, we'd better learn quickly how to respond to our common noncompliance cited in letter A! Given our current, more broadly representative religious base, Adam's original sin isn't the frequent topic it once was in English class, but the energetically grim foundation upon which we base academics in this country remains subliminally intact.[133]

A forward-thinking neurologist-turned-schoolteacher, Judy Willis, MD, has (thankfully!) spent much of her double career studying how

---

132 Seriously? This is how children learned their first letters? I'm not sure I understand what that Y rhyme even means!
133 Fortunately, the system is flooded with loving, kind educators who care deeply about students and bring joy to their classrooms.

children learn best. It turns out that "best" doesn't come from sitting still and reciting rotely, or even feeling like a foolish sinner. According to Willis, "brain research tells us that when the fun stops, learning often stops too." In her insightful article "The Neuroscience of Joyful Education," Dr. Willis writes this:

> When students are engaged and motivated and feel minimal stress, information flows freely through the affective filter in the amygdala and they achieve higher levels of cognition, make connections, and experience "aha" moments. Such learning comes not from quiet classrooms and directed lectures, but from classrooms with an atmosphere of exuberant discovery (Kohn, 2004).[134]

Because "exuberant discovery" is more innately true about us than "stressed out," it is easy to understand that learning in a joyful—centered—state would naturally be more productive. There is at least one school in my own town, the Khabele School, that begins each middle- and high-school class with a few moments for centering. The administration tells us that these preclass exercises help "focus the classroom on learning as well as increase student performance on presentations and tests." Wow, now there's a thought: get centered—be in the middle of your inherent joy—so you have more space to learn and remember! They also offer gardening classes to the youngest of students and hold many of their classes outside. Seems like they "get" the joy and learning connection.

The workplace is another venue we somehow decided early on should be funereally unfun. Led largely by American high-tech companies, however, the trend is shifting more toward the joy⇔creativity⇔financial success equation. A recent employee survey of the top twenty-five companies to work for highlights the fact that fun and connectedness are major positive attributes. And from their corporate annual reports, the bottom line

---

134 You can read the whole article at ASCD.org in the Summer 2007 edition, volume 64.

seems to appreciate a little jolly companionship as well! Here is a sampling of the companies:

Twitter: Besides connecting folks with some 500 million Tweets a day, this company also encourages employees to volunteer. Then there are the Northern California rooftop team meetings…

Progressive Insurance: Even I, a person who almost never watches TV, have seen those funny, irreverent commercials Progressive produces. Word from the inside is that Progressive is filled with "amazing" employees and has a good work-life-balance perspective.

Disneyland: Need I really elaborate? Isn't it called the most magical place on earth?

Nike: I'll bet if Nike were in charge of education, PE would never be kicked off the curriculum! Besides the perks of cool shoes and an awesome HQ campus, this company lives up to its goal of fostering "a culture of invention." (And its fair-trade issues seem to have greatly improved.)

Apple: Isn't Apple just another word for "cool" or "awesome"?

Intuit (tax and accounting software and services): How impressive is it that an accounting-based company makes it to the top twenty-five! One of the employees described part of the awesomeness as "We care and give back."

Southwest Airlines: Have you been on a SWA flight lately? If so, you may have heard the following:

> "And we want to thank you for choosing Southwest. We know you have a lot of choices, and we're so glad the others are all so expensive."

(*Upon hitting some turbulence.*) "No need to be alarmed, folks. That was just the sound of your luggage being ejected from the aircraft."

(*As the plane arrived at the gate and people began standing up while the seat belt light was still illuminated.*) "We need help cleaning the lavatories, so please stand up if you can pitch in."

Doesn't it always seem like Southwest Airlines employees are enjoying themselves? I'm so thankful that all these companies (and more, certainly) are demonstrating that success and fun can cohabit in delightful, financially profitable ways.

⌒

Into eternity, where all is one,
there crept a tiny, mad idea,
at which the Son of God remembered
not to laugh.

—*A Course in Miracles*,
T-27.VIII.6.2

⌒

In addition to employers making the workplace more fun-centric, researchers are now confirming that employees who have more fun—can you say vacation?—are better employees! People who take time off from work actually up the office morale, feel happier, and are more productive when they *are* at work (creating higher employee retention), and they are physically healthier (vacation misers are shown to be more likely to suffer cardiovascular disease). Yet, according to Project Time Off, Americans leave some 429 *million* vacation days on the table each year!

With striking irony, we even take on a deadly earnestness in meditation. Often, when we meditate or pray, we approach such acts with incredible seriousness, as if laughter or silliness would kill our Zen mojo. *Au contraire!* The animal kingdom is filled with examples of staying in centeredness while, apparently, having a good time. Do butterflies look like they are brooding? Do sea lions ever look somber? And then, we can't forget to consider those lilies![135] Yet nonseriousness doesn't seem to be the current MO for many a meditative mission. I once spent an entire day in a silent meditation retreat sitting soundlessly for a certain gong-prescribed time; circumvolving the temple perimeter, lips closed, head down, step, step, stepping; eating wordlessly; all according to the schedule. I witnessed not one smile the entire day (I compliantly adhered to the no-smile protocol, not wanting to ruin the mood that was set). After all, we weren't there to be happy; we were there to become more spiritual! While it was lovely to enjoy some silence and be surrounded by people who were truly trying to find their center, I have to admit that all that glum calm didn't make me feel even a nanometer closer to Love.

That was not, of course, the only setting I've witnessed seriousness trumping spontaneity and simple joy. I've come across many situations that confuse being spiritually devoted with being stone-faced solemn; in fact, I've been overseer of a few myself! And though I'm really not certain how we got this way (we can't blame it entirely on *The New England Primer*), I am certain it's time to take a different tact. We would do ourselves a big honkin' favor to habituate joy. Fortunately, there are uncountable ways to do this.

---

135 This is a reference to one of my favorite passages in the Bible, Luke 12:27, "Consider the lilies, how they grow: they neither toil nor spin, yet I tell you, even Solomon in all his glory was not arrayed like one of these."

Melancholy is the poison of devotion.

—CLARE OF ASSISI

We start, as always, with ourselves. Ask yourself a few pertinent questions. For example:

1. Are you anyone *you* would seek out at a party? Do conversations with you leave people smiling, or have you made sure everyone knows about the terrible experience you had on your last flight to Houston?
2. Are you a delightful family member, or have you assigned yourself the job of Family Taskmaster?[136]
3. Do you have people over, even if your house is messy?
4. Do you hear yourself saying "Yes!" more often than "No"?
5. Do you wonder at life, marvel at the daily stuff?
6. Do you spend time blessing-counting? (I find that the act of closing my eyes and counting my blessings automatically turns up the corners of my mouth!)
7. Do you play games with your friends/kids/spouse?
8. Do you volunteer your time?
9. Do you ever donate money?
10. Do you get outside much?
11. Do you find a lot to laugh about?
12. Do you dance in the middle of the grocery aisle? OK, that may be going a bit too far for many folks, but if you haven't tried it, you may want to consider at least twirling around in the privacy of your own home. I can still get my youngest son to dance with me

---

136 I tried that position for quite a while: no time off, and "employees" give you stink eye and/or try to avoid you. Besides, it's no fun at all!

to a good song, and we always find big smiles from just a little time kicking up our heels!

If you answered yes to most of these, then hooray! You probably have an open-door policy for joy.

If "Uhhhmmm, no" was your predominant response, then maybe this is a good time to become more aware of your role as conscious, joy-filled life liver. Because we are all in charge of our own lives (and therefore happiness), the good news is that we can invite more joy in *today*! Here are some quick 'n' easy suggestions:

1. Pull out your board games—or maybe playing cards—and invite the neighbors over, even if your home is a disaster. Everyone will be having such a good time that nobody will even notice the schmutz on the floor or the dust on the piano. Some of my family's favorites are Apples to Apples, Set, Pit, Codenames, and Mexican Train.
2. Fork over about $10 or so for a table-tennis set and clip it on to your kitchen table (if your table isn't round...or maybe even if it is round!). When we stretched a thin mesh net across our own table, it added a shocking amount of fun to our lives. We can volley before school, during study breaks, when friends come over... anytime, really (though we do remove the place mats first!). The games are generally accompanied by plenty of smack talk and laughter.

   There was a time when the thought of turning a primary piece of furniture, located in the very center of my house, into a Ping-Pong table would have *horrified* me. Now I realize that such prime real estate just invites everyone to play and connect. The table-as-Ping-Pong base offers many more smiles now than ever before!

There are benefits other than just laughter to table tennis. Dr. Daniel G. Amen, brain guru, says that Ping-Pong is the "world's best brain sport." The hand-eye logistics, focus, strategizing, and planning are all good for different parts of our brains. And, as an additional benefit, concussions are almost unheard of in this sport!

3. Learn to juggle—I mean with balls, not schedules, kids, and work—because we already do that anyway. For people more coordinated than I am, learning can take less than an hour. Interestingly, this fun activity is *also* good for brains (it increases the area of our brains devoted to visual memory) and coordination, and adds greatly to our party-going popularity.

4. Take a walk. Even if it's raining or snowing, meandering among the birds, grass, and trees has all sorts of benefits. Lots of studies speak to nature's positive influence on ADHD, vision, measurable stress reduction, and other body related improvements. But really, if we simply notice how we *feel* when we are outside, we will recognize the benefits—and sheer joy of it, without requiring research!

5. Call someone you haven't spoken with in a while who has made a big difference in your life. Or write a letter. Let her know you appreciate/Love her! Because giving and receiving are the same thing, you'll be adding a double dose of joy to the world.

6. Let smiling be your daily meditation.

7. Have your own Yes! Day.[137] My children would prefer *every* day be a Yes! Day. Although I haven't been able to work that out completely yet (Yes! Days for them mostly orbit around incessant electronical use and ice cream bonanzas), I find that consciously yessing my way through a day helps me realize all the times I unthinkingly say no to possibilities.[138]

---

137 We adopted this idea from the darling book, *Yes Day!*, written by Amy Krouse and illustrated by Tom Lichtenheld.

138 It turns out that I'm not the slightest bit nondual (yet) when it comes to unfettered screen time…good information to know!

8. If you don't already have one, find a funny friend, or two, or twenty. Fortunately, several grace my own life and gift me with laughter on a regular basis. For instance, all I have to do is receive a text from my entertaining, incredibly Love-filled friend Shawna, and even before I read it, I'm laughing (I know what's coming: she's *hilarious*). You can imagine, then, how laughter pervades her actual presence.

   And looping around for a minute to the point about joy and learning, I'll add that both of my children were fortunate to have Shawna teach them in elementary school. One day, my youngest insightfully pointed out, "You know, Mom, it's funny. Teacher A is super serious and always yells at us. Nobody even likes to go into her classroom because we're always worried we'll get in trouble. Teacher B gets off track so easily that one minute she'll be talking about social studies, and the next minute, she's talking about ice cream. But when I had Mrs. P. for my teacher, we always laughed and danced and had tons of fun...*and* I learned more in her class than any other one!"

9. Give yourself the day off from bossing your kids and/or spouse and/or friends around—twenty-four whole hours of "being OK with." If you feel your tyrannical streak plotting to overtake your resolve, excuse yourself and Google "funny joke," or stand on your head, or sing your favorite song! You always have any number of options besides demanding that your family behave in a certain way—*your* way. You will *all* feel stress relief from this practice!

10. Create a "happy songs" playlist, and listen to it frequently. Some tunes on our happy playlist include "Give Me Back My Wig" by Hound Dog Taylor, "Some Days You Gotta Dance" by the Dixie Chicks, Israel Kamakawiwo'ole's version of "Somewhere over the Rainbow," "Living in the Moment" by Jason Mraz, "Peanut Butter Jelly Time" by DJ Chipman, "Beautiful Day" by U2, "Happy" by

Pharrell Williams, and, of course, "Everything Is Awesome" by Tegan and Sara of *The Lego Movie.*

Bottom line: don't put off joy! You can see how much it helps us: the "should" side of us wins, and the "Love" side of us wins! Every time.

And anyway, our bodies love it when we smile. Studies have proven[139] that even a *fake* smile causes us to pump out endorphins (those "feel good" hormones) and to decrease adrenaline (the hormone that floods into our bodies when we perceive a "fight or flight" situation). On average, kids naturally smile about four hundred times each and every day, so they regularly offer themselves huge doses of endorphins! The average grown-up seems to muster only about twenty smile-produced endorphin hits daily.

A Few Reasons to Smile
(according to the experts):

* We are perceived as more attractive.
* Destressing hormones are released, which could lead to better memory.
* We live longer.
* We feel less pain.
* We're happier and less anxious than frowners are.

---

139 I know I'm doing things a bit backward—again—to justify joy by bolstering it with studies! Well, we do love our "proof," so until we internalize the regular feelings of joy, I'll continue to exploit our addiction to facts and what the experts say.

Even before any smile and happiness research came out, Jesus made a really worthwhile point (as usual) when he recommended that we act like little kids. "Truly I tell you, unless you change and become like little children, you will never enter the kingdom of heaven."[140] I'm pretty sure he wasn't talking about the occasional tantrum, but the smiling part. The endorphin part. The naturally living in joy part. That *is* our kingdom of heaven!

How often we find our way there is a matter of being aware. Thankfully, once again, my family members have volunteered as my very own life-lesson prompters. This time, it was my husband who inadvertently helped me find my way to greater insight.

Bob is a fabulous amateur photographer. He chronicles our children in ways that render surplus the words I write about them (but I persist because they *are* my favorite topic). He squints regularly behind his lens, documenting moments. And interestingly, one of the valuable lessons his lens has taught me is that *they are all valuable moments*! Laughing at the dinner table. Diving into the pool. Holidays. Haircuts. School activities. Each moment is worth appreciating and celebrating. It's really helpful to remember the joy present in the "ordinary" times!

Unfortunately—or make that *fortunately*—his lens has offered me insights about myself that I may never have noticed were it not for its ubiquity. Because of its always-thereness, I long ago developed a form of inattentional blindness to the picture-taking thing. I often don't even notice my husband snapping memories, a case made evident as I glanced through our 4,322,007 photos over the past few years.

---

140 Matthew 8:13.

⟨⟩

The aim of life is to live, and to live means to be aware;
joyously,
drunkenly,
serenely,
divinely
aware.

—HENRY MILLER

⟨⟩

Frequently in this collection of images, I am in the background, persevering with my busyness. What I noticed in past pictures was a definite tension, or uncalled-for seriousness, in my body and face, aka unconsciousness amid joy! So busy was I organizing and making things "perfect" that I blatantly neglected the happiness sparkling all around me.

For example, one fall, when we were a host family to a Chinese student, we invited other hosted students and their American families over for a party. The theme—because it was around Thanksgiving and I *really* love a theme—was "pretzel-shaped thankfulness." Everyone was to form his or her gratitude using pretzel dough as the medium. It was hilarious! The shapes were surprisingly varied, incredibly creative, and delicious. I loved it. *But*, reviewing the pictures from the party, amid rich imaginations, boiling water, and laughter, I could see "hostess stiffness" all over my face. Aiming for the "perfect party," I missed basking in every minute of the talented togetherness. (I actually thought I had been enjoying every minute until the photos disabused me.) Shocking.

When the photos alerted me to what I surely did not want to repeat, I didn't say, "Shame on me!" I know now (though I didn't always know) that such shame does *not* serve me. What I have done, instead, is find gratitude in the knowing-nowness and ferry that information to subsequent host-essing gigs, along with a heightened consciousness of joy in the thick of mess and mayhem.

EXERCISE 20: Photographic Memory

GO FOR IT!

OK, wanna see if you are plugged in while you *aren't* sitting with your timer? While you're "just" living life? Then walk down Memory Lane via your photo albums (or piles of pictures in shoe boxes), and notice if the images align with your memory of the situation.

1. Sit down with some old pictures or videos that include you (selfies don't really count for this exercise). Are you in the middle of the fun? Are you off on the sidelines? Are you missing completely (because you are ironing the napkins, wiping off the counters, or sitting in the corner with your head focused on your cell phone)?
2. If you find, as I did, that the four-by-six image is not the "picture of presence" you would like to create for yourself, please do it now. Take three-ish minutes and imagine being in situations in which the only thing that matters is having a great time with the people you Love—not the table being set, not being bummed because dinner burned or the guest of honor is an hour late…not any other detail but joy. Prime yourself.
3. The next time you are hosting a party or a meeting, or just being part of a group, imagine bringing total presence and awareness with you. Any camera will bear honest witness to your new perspective.

Imagine how delightful it will be to look through the pictures years from now and remember all that fun—complete with photographic proof that you were engaged and enjoying yourself all along the way!

GIVING JOY

One of the most indispensable, primary, beautiful ingredients to a happy life is knowing how to give. Maybe that sounds sanctimonious, or ridiculously evident, but it's a truth backed up—yet again!—by those fabulous researchers and experts who seem to be pruning the fact trail for my every belief! Yes, for years researchers have been conducting studies that statistically prove what we can all feel: *givers are happier people*. Using all manner of graphs, charts, and data, experts from Harvard to UC Berkeley report that "prosocial spending" (known to the rest of us as donating money for a good cause) satisfies core human requirements and so promotes a greater degree of happiness and satisfaction to the giver. Like I said, givers are happier people.

When we donate money,
our nucleus accumbens-
the part of our brains that re-
leases dopamine-
lights up in a way very similarly
to when we eat chocolate
or fall in love.

But it's not just in spending spondulicks that happiness, life satisfaction, and even health measures all receive a boost. When we share our time and attention for no other overt reason than to help another soul, increased happiness gets reported across the board. So why don't more of us do more of it? Probably because so many of us are such devout believers in scarcity: we presume there is a limited amount of good stuff, and if we give *our* piece of the good-gtuff pie away—especially that most "precious" commodity, time—we won't have enough for ourselves.

Who came up with that pie thing, anyway?

Perhaps the dour but quite influential political economist, Thomas Malthus, contributed to that philosophy when, in 1798, he published this thought:[141]

> The power of population is so superior to the power of the earth to produce subsistence for man, that premature death must in some shape or other visit the human race...gigantic inevitable famine stalks in the rear, and with one mighty blow levels the population with the food of the world.[142]

In Malthusian summary: too many people trying to snag the limited-resources pie surely means doom for all. I guess he hadn't heard the one about necessity being the mother of invention. Or, moreover, the story of Stone Soup.

Research today suggests stonesoupology as a way of recovering our natural abundance. Dr. Christian Smith, who runs the University of Notre Dame's Science of Generosity Initiative, has spent much of his career understanding how sharing affects us in extremely positive ways. In his intelligent book *The Paradox of Generosity: Giving We Receive, Grasping We Lose*, he explains the concept:

---

141 Malthus's ideas were quite powerful in his day. Darwin credits this very essay with helping him establish his ideas on natural selection.

142 Thomas Malthus, *An Essay on the Principle of Population, as it Affects the Future Improvement of Society with Remarks on the Speculations of Mr. Godwin, M. Condorcet, and Other Writers*, page 44, London, Printed for J. Johnson, in St. Paul's Church-Yard, 1798.

Those who give their resources away, receive back in return... In letting go some of what we own for the good of others, we better secure our own lives, too. This paradox of generosity is a sociological fact, confirmed by evidence drawn from quantitative surveys and qualitative interviews.[143]

I love that there's an enterprise devoted to generosity and that smart, insightful people are conducting "respectable" research on the subject. To their body of work, I would like to add my position that *giving feels good because it acknowledges our interconnectedness.* Buddhism teaches this idea—All Is One—so, as usual, I'm saying absolutely nothing new. Saint Francis felt completely connected to animals and all of nature. The Sufis, physicists, and a host of others throughout history have supported the notion that we are all connected. But you don't even have to believe in interconnectedness to benefit from giving, according to academics and research!

**Too many have dispensed with generosity
in order to practice charity.**

—Albert Camus

I know people who are born givers, like my sister, Katy, and my soul sister, Catherine. Those of us not born with the giving gift are fortunate that some folks came knowing this stuff; we can learn a lot from their organically openhearted way of being. Generosity for Katy and Catherine is *instinctual.* I know they arrived on this planet more naturally generous

---

143 Christian Smith and Hilary Davidson, *The Paradox of Generosity: Giving We Receive, Grasping We Lose* (Oxford University Press, 2014) 224.

than I am, for instance, because they each *still* surprise me with their automatic kindnesses. I continuously watch and learn…and feel very grateful for what they have to teach me.

For example, my nephew spent a week in a serious burn unit,[144] and my sister (who spent the week with him, sleeping on fold-out chairs and eating a fair share of hospital cafeteria food) "adopted" the family across the hall. In the middle of her own grueling experience, she inspired my nephew's school to rally behind a fire-damaged family unknown to her prior to their mutual scorchedness. My sister turned her dark experience into a blessing for others. Typical.

Also typical of my sweet sister is the focus she chooses during any challenges life flings in her direction. Throughout my nephew's recovery (and during other times), a phrase I heard repeatedly from my sister was "I am strong." I never witnessed her complain or bemoan. I did, however, hear her express unwaning gratefulness for the doctors, the hospital administration, the firefighters, my nephew's teachers, and her family and friends who offered such incredible support. Not one peep of "poor-me-ness."

The only reason I know Catherine volunteers at least twenty hours a week is because I try regularly to align our schedules so we can laugh and walk together, while she simultaneously inspires me (she is quick-witted *and* brilliant). Casual Catherine-knowers, however, would not be privy to information about the tireless energy and brainpower she shares regularly with the world because she never mentions it. (I pry it out of her.) Whether she is protecting children through the legal system, serving as the "track mom" when nobody else wants the job, or making an unscheduled taco delivery to the *entire* lacrosse team so that not one boy will be hungry (rather than just bringing one for her own son), this woman thinks of ways to give, give, give.

---

144 I am grateful to report that he has no long-term physical damage!

She always finds the joy too. If a situation turns out not quite "ideal," Catherine is the first to point out that it could have been worse. By consciously facing her perspective the direction of the good, she can't attest to (or promote) the bad, *and* she can elect to feel happy about all the details in her life. Oh, and the word I hear her use most often to describe herself? "Lucky—I'm just very lucky."

One of the biggest charitable pointers I've gleaned from standing back and watching these two sisters of mine in action is that they cannot, literally, see a different way. Whether saving stray dogs (and cats and bunnies), or driving the Mobile Loaves and Fishes truck on a regular basis, they each reflexively and modestly orient themselves toward giving. If I've unthinkingly asked one or the other why she did a certain something, more often than not, she responds with either a "that did not compute" blank stare (as in "What? There's another option besides generosity? I didn't know that!") or a nonchalance that implies that that particular instance of giving was no more an external thought than breathing.

For those of us who still find giving a less-than-innate response (and who would like to experience the documented happiness giving can offer while simultaneously making the world a sweeter place), I'll share an experiment that felt very powerful for me. Fortunately, it proves that we don't need to start by volunteering twenty hours a week or adopting entire families in need.[145] We can start with little things,[146] and end up being amazed by how big they feel!

I tried the following practice, thanks to the inspiration of a man I loved very, very much. Jack was one of the most life-living, "big" human beings I've ever been lucky enough to know, and his incredible example and support changed the course of my life. I was aware, certainly, that many

---

145 Though we certainly *could*. Don't let my suggestions stop you from your own great plans!
146 We may call things "little," but there's no "little" when it comes to extending Love.

people loved him too, but it wasn't until I attended his funeral, where, gathered in a single space, were so many others whose lives had been similarly, beautifully changed, that I realized the magnitude of his generosity. At one point, Jack's youngest son considered asking how many in the room had lived at his parents' house. We looked around and realized that about 99.9 percent of the people under fifty-five would have raised their hands (myself included). Who lets that many people squat at their house? Jack and his creative, fun and inspiring wife, Kären, certainly.

True generosity:
You give your all,
and yet you always feel as if it costs you nothing.

—Simone de Beauvoir

Feeling gratefully inspired, I decided to be intentionally more like Jack and Kären: to open my heart and home in ways that make people feel Loved. Here's what it looked like (what it felt like—beyond fabulous—is not possible for me to put into words).

EXERCISE 21: Jack It Up

GO FOR IT!

Jack's generosity and full-throttle living went hand in hand, a fact I recalled while listening to so many people recite the kindnesses (and hilarity) he'd shelled out during his life. It made me wonder just how many kindnesses *I* had been scattering on such a regular, automatic basis. I quickly concluded that I was way behind schedule in the generosity department. So I resolved to spend the next 365 days doing something out-of-my-way nice for others— strangers, friends, family—it did not matter. I didn't expect I'd be inviting people to live in our house (though I didn't preclude that option), but I did plan to wake up daily, intent on giving.

So, for one year, every single day, I made it my conscious mission to do something extra-kind for someone. The delights were really all mine: it was fun to wake up each morning plotting some form of outgoing compassion. I can definitely say it changed my own awareness about giving, and, wow, did it make *me* happy to bring even a smidge of comfort, peace, or joy into someone's life. While I cannot say I've reached the leagues of Jack, Kären, Katy, and Catherine, I am closer than I was, and that feels incredible!

1. Mark your calendar because this will be a special day in your life. (I started on the first day of a new year, so it was easy to remember; but don't wait for a notable day—start as soon as you can!) You don't need to announce this to anyone, by the way, and the recipients don't even need to know you were the giver.[147]
2. When you wake up in the morning, think of something Loving to do for another being (the givee doesn't have to be a human). It could be shoveling snow for your neighbor or giving a total stranger your sandwich for lunch. If you can't determine something specific in advance, at least you've started the day off with the *intention* of seeking out an opportunity to give. That alone will likely ensure that you get the chance. Watch for that chance. Invite it in, and it will not fail to show up for you.
3. Commit an act of generosity. Any act of generosity.

---

147 Because I believe we are all connected, giving and receiving are the very same thing. So any delineation between "giver" and "receiver" is moot, anyway!

4. Before you go to sleep, consider what you did. It will prob-
    ably bring a smile to your face and a warm feeling to your
    own heart's center.
5. Repeat this for the following 364 days, when you will find
    yourself in a place of greater joy, having thought about
    others so consistently. This I can promise!

After the experiment is finished, you'll likely find yourself automatically creating—and delighting in—ways to continue "outgoing" niceties
(because now you know how fabulous they make you feel!).

All these kinds of giving bring an understanding with them. It's that
connectedness thing again. Giving feels so good because it reminds us of
our intertwined nature, which is our truth. In aligning with that truth,
it bears repeating, that it's always the *how* (with Love) not the *what* (what
amount of money we give or the number of hours we donate at the local
fund-raiser) that matters.

LOUD SMILES

Joy really *is* a better measurement of spiritual congruence than pretty
much anything else (it beats a hair shirt every time). A sure sign we are in
the vicinity of connectedness is to note how much fun we are having in
the moment (even before a camera catches us). If something doesn't feel
good, we are probably far from our center. Of course, your fun and my fun
might live in completely different time zones and bear little resemblance,
which is a valuable thing to note. Joy, after all, comes in uncountable sizes
and flavors. I've felt radical joy in my garden, surrounded by my dearly
loved roses and herb blossoms. I have stood in their midst, eyes closed, and
breathed what truly felt like pure, heavenly, silent joy.

More frequently, though, joy finds its way to me in openmouthed, high-
decibel laughter. One is not superior to the other, not at all. And it's valuable

to recognize that each person experiences joy differently. Everyone expresses joy at the perfect level for the individual. In fact, if I ever witnessed my husband high-fiving the air and giggling like I do, I would probably think something was wrong with him! But that doesn't mean he isn't happy. He's a different happy. (Sometimes when we watch shows that make me roar, I ask him why he's not laughing. He assures me that he's laughing inside.)

We can each create our own kind of fun-o-meter to let us know if we're on track—anything that can help us stop to consider how much joy we allow, and then "scatter," as Emerson suggested. My best measurer is laughter. While I am not a funny person, I *can* boast top-notch laughing skills, so my daily quantity and quality of laughter help me understand where I am in relation to my truth.

Whether we are generally loud or silent about our joy, laughter is, for most of us, a delightful way to confirm that we are in the neighborhood of connectedness. How often do you actively seek out reasons or ways to laugh more? If the answer is "Not a lot," then here are a few ideas:

EXERCISE 22: Laugh a Lot

GO FOR IT!

Because smiling does such wonders for us, biologically and in every other way, I imagine that laughing is the caffeinated version of silently lifting the corners of our mouths. I've yet to see a study that pits smiling against laughing in the benefits department, but judging from how I feel after I've had a good giggle, I'm pretty sure we can't go wrong by encouraging a little (or a lot) more har-de-har to our lives.

Instead of the news, daringly watch a funny movie! There are zillions, old and new. On the Internet, on TV, on DVDs at the library. There are so many sources of movie laughter!

Or read a funny book. Any of these authors always make me chuckle (and not just on the inside!):

* Anne Lamott
* Calvin Trillin
* Tina Fey
* Dr. Seuss
* Nora Ephron
* Mark Twain
* David Sedaris
* So many more

And if you don't have time for a show or an entire book, look up funny videos! The Internet can easily provide uncountable reasons to laugh in two- or three-minute segments. View snippets of Jimmy Fallon's, or Ellen's[148] shows before breakfast, and laugh right along with them! Look up videos of James Corden's Carpool Karaoke, parrots laughing like supervillains or kids giving the evil eye...there are zillions to choose from. No time for a video? Google "funny boxer dog pictures" and just look for a minute. I dare you not to laugh!

I frequently get in bed mentally reviewing the funny things that happened during my day and doze off laughing (which I'll bet is vibrationally similar to gratitude and prayer!).

At dinner, I usually ask my family members what made them laugh during the day. It is a much better question than "How was your day?"[149] It's a memory everyone feels good about sharing, and I love watching smiles cross my sons' faces as they recall the joy. Besides, it helps my kids invite funny things in.

148 How awesome is it that Love-filled people like these joy spreaders make it their *jobs* to help us remember to laugh! I'm so grateful for them. (Wouldn't it be awesome to sit between Jimmy and Ellen at a dinner party?)

149 I've tried that one too, but it can so often result in monosyllabic disappointment! "Good" and "Fine" deny me the details I enjoy!

Finally, laughter is a wonderful response to many situations that might otherwise seize our egos. When we are angry about something, it's really our out-of-alignment ego getting in the way of our natural joy. But if we choose laughter over frothing at the mouth, we can acknowledge to ourselves the real unimportance of anything that doesn't resemble happiness. I mean, really, is a poor driver, an unemptied dishwasher, or a late appointment really worth alienating joy over?

For example, the other day, my oldest son and I were talking about this very book being almost ready for prime time. "I'm glad you're doing that, Mom," he said, deeply sincere. "It finally gives some meaning to your life." What? Did he just say my life needed more meaning? I could hardly stop laughing! While I have adored writing this book, and am so thankful that another soul might possibly benefit from—or at the very least, enjoy—all these years I've been "repenting" and attempting to remember Love, my life has *never*, for a nanosecond, been without "meaning."[150] How absolutely hilarious to perceive any life is deemed to have meaning only by doing something that others can judge, measure, or at least know about. As if being the most Loving, happy person I could possibly be—while schlepping my kids, cooking dinners, volunteering, and even running a company or two—could all be somehow less valuable than writing a book![151]

There was a time, however, when that statement would have offended me. My ego, previously agreeing with the metrics the rest of the world employs, would have scoffed, pouted, and perhaps even yelled some explanation back. But now, mostly being happy-no-matter-what—taking joy "seriously"—I found no responsive anger, only laughter. And it seems laughter is a most appropriate response when we *do* take joy seriously!

---

150 *Nobody's* life is without meaning! We are all integral parts of the whole. We are *all* necessary, valuable, and treasured!

151 And, truthfully, I could never have written this book were it not for my kids, the cooking, the schlepping, the work—all of it!

CHAPTER 12

Only the Beginning!

Once you make a decision,
the universe conspires to make it happen.

—Ralph Waldo Emerson

Deep within you is everything that is perfect,
ready to radiate through you and out into the world.

—*A Course in Miracles*,
W-pI.41.3:1

I LIKE A BOOK WITH a happy ending, but this is different. Not different in the "happy," but different in the "ending"; this is *not* an ending. Now that we have—hopefully—invited new thoughts to our world, we can *know* that every moment is really a perfect invitation to boundless possibilities! If we haven't felt that limitless Love all around us yet, we are, at the very least, closer to believing it's already here. It's waiting tolerantly[152] to fork over more joy than we've ever been able to imagine and experience. Ever. All we have to do is stay awake and be ready to receive. And that's easier because we've been practicing throughout this entire book…right?

---

152 It never actually left us, despite our insistence to the contrary!

As we have seen in the previous chapters, *probably the most important aspect of staying awake and open to the everywhen awesomeness of Love is remaining vigilant to our thought choices.* We each entertain somewhere between fifty thousand and seventy thousand thoughts every single day, so vigilance might seem like a tall order. But we've already taken custody of uncountable thoughts by starting the day intentionally, as well as injecting awareness throughout various daily activities. We also know that we can alter our perception to see things differently: we are *much* closer to mastery than we ever have been!

We are what we repeatedly do.
Excellence, then,
is not an act, but a habit.

—ARISTOTLE

So now I'd like to share another tip to help keep those 50K-ish notions, judgments, internal deliberations, troubles, and whimsies of ours on track. It is a powerful way of iterating our thoughts to better serve us on a daily—or moment-by-moment—basis. This is really the ultimate jelly plug-in:

EXERCISE 23: Thought Watch

GO FOR IT!

Throughout this book, we've taken "time apart" to focus on changing our thoughts, our perspectives, and our beliefs through peanut-butter-and-jelly-like plug-ins. This exercise goes further, leaving no possibility for nonjoy to leak through any cracks of inattention.

Those experts tell us that the daily fifty thousand to seventy thousand thoughts we produce are mostly all the same. This is really good news in the Joy Department, now that we've taken changing our minds to the next level. Instead of letting the thoughts think us, we can confidently take charge and, with awareness, determine the quality of our every thought (and with that, control the quality of our lives.)

1. Choose a phrase or two with which you'd like to replace some of those thousands of other thoughts hurtling through your brain, unconsciously creating your version of the world. Here are some suggestions. Use any or all of them…or choose your own. (Just select ones that you can actually *feel* when you say them!)

    —I am joy-filled.   —Awesomeness abounds in me.
    —I'm radically radiant.   —I'm divinely delighted.
    —I am peaceful.   —I'm luminous.
    —I am blessed.   —I remember my truth.
    —I remember who I am.   —I am a Love virtuoso.
    —Big Love is my real name.   —I'm awake.
    —I'm glorious.   —My Source is always with me.
    —Joy is my truth.   —I am Love.
    —I am present.   —I'm perfectly aligned.

2. Now run that thought through your noggin, set your ever-helpful timer for ten minutes, and carry on. When ten minutes have sped by (hopefully with fewer and fewer leftover thoughts), restate whatever phrase(s) you are using.

Let me be clear: I'm not suggesting that you meditate for ten minutes on your selected phrase; I'm suggesting that you insert the thought *once* among the other thoughts recycling through your grey matter and go about your life. Then consciously insert the phrase(s) again ten minutes later.

3. Repeat this all day long. (Perhaps you can set your timer to vibrate so the rest of your household members and/or colleagues don't develop their own thoughts about strangling the person who keeps beeping!) Right, that's no typo: every ten minutes, retrain your brain with truthful thoughts *you* select, rather than thoughts your history, the radio, a clever billboard campaign, or your grandmother's guilt chose on your behalf when you weren't paying attention. Repeat as needed on subsequent days, and enjoy your new level of Love's awareness!

⸻

As a single footstep will not make a path on the earth, so a single thought will not make a pathway in the mind. To make a deep physical path, we walk again and again. To make a deep mental path, we must think over and over the kind of thoughts we wish to dominate our lives.

—Henry David Thoreau

⸻

The exercise above[153] does amazing things for creating "a deep mental path" to the joy we so often temporarily ignore or forget altogether. In

---

153 I adapted it from Lesson 40 of *A Course in Miracles*.

other words, it helps us cultivate our awareness of the right here, right now. It puts us smack-dab in the present instant, which is exactly where we belong. Plain and beautifully simple. Because as we now know, *focusing on the beauty of now keeps the fear of not-now from creating a roadblock to joy*.[154]

BEING WONDER-FULL

When we can get to the very moment we are in, we usually find that it leads us back to our wonder. The wonder I'm talking about has nothing to do with confusion over why your brother-in-law can never show up to family dinners on time. This kind of wonder is about inviting the delights that jump into our open arms when we stay awake and curious, as we've been practicing throughout this book. The closer we get to our true selves—no longer dragging around those hefty, outdated, and probably not maximally joy-filled thoughts—the more we'll find ourselves hanging out in wonder. In the wonder of now, we are so busy with our own awesome activities that we forget to feel awful about how we compare to the Joneses or the Jhandupurs or the Smellingtons. We don't need to get out our deficiency tape measure. In wonder, we can easily suspend judgment and criticism, not by trying to block them out, but because we are so focused on flinging open the door, letting open-eyed gladness roll in and make itself right at home, where it belongs. *Wonder is an attitude, an approach to life. Joy is where it takes us, our true selves.*

Awareness ☞ Wonder ☞ Our True Joy

Think about this concept with me for a minute, and it will make total sense, especially if you remember your childhood or have been in the presence of children lately. Children remember this equation. Mostly, they

---

154 Not schlepping fear of what might in the future and anger of what was in the past gives us so more room in our brains to realize the now of it all!

live this equation! That is, until we start noosing them with rules and "shoulds" (as in: you should always make your bed and clean your plate), having them measure themselves against others (what are grades in school if not a comparison to what the other kids know according to standards some expert or politician established?), and forgetting to honor their innate interestedness ("Don't touch that!" "Don't interrupt!"). By the time we are adults, our equation becomes agonizingly inverted, and our truth gets thwarted by uncountable prohibitions to wonder or be curious (wonder and curiosity are twins, or at the very least, first cousins). This sure zaps a lot of possibilities for self-awareness, or self-remembering. In her glorious book *The Color Purple*, Alice Walker perfectly expressed it like this: "The more I wonder, the more I love."

Wonder is the spark that lights up our truth.

My longtime friend Allyson is a close acquaintance of wonder. She constantly marvels at and with her kids, her community, her friends, books, politicians, and even magazine articles. Her openhearted perspective leads her to wonder on a regular basis. There are other grown-ups in my life who also deeply inspire me with their ability to be (or fall, or leap, depending on how you look at it) in wonder: Jenn, Maxine, Bashar, Tina, David, Shannon, Paul, and Dave, for instance. When I am with them—when I even *think* about them—I am reminded of the exuberance that sparkles in remembering to be wonder-full.

You may not know these particular wonder-fulls, so I'll point out some more well-known folks who (though I've never met any of them in person) seem very wonder-driven to me: Nelson Mandela, Elizabeth Gilbert, Benjamin

Franklin, Mary Oliver, Rhett and Link, Isabel Allende, Sir Ken Robinson, Maya Angelou, Ellen DeGeneres, Leonardo da Vinci, Alice Waters, Casey Neistat, Wangari Maathai, and the ever-curious Albert Einstein.

I wonder what's going to happen exciting today?

—PIGLET

To taste a little wonder for yourself right now, just conjure the image of a child's wide-eyed response to seeing a puppy for the first time. That's wonder-filled, isn't it? And when was the last time you felt that kind of wonder? I hope it was as recent as this morning, when you first heard the birds serenading you, because wonder is a state of mind that invites grace. It's the mind-set we've been retraining throughout this book! If wonder has been eluding you still, here are some ideas to help you bask in "incomparable wonder."

EXERCISE 24: Ways to Stay Wonder-Full

GO FOR IT!

I promise this is not a bait and switch, but as much as I'd like to give you the abracadabra of wonder, you will have to develop your own actual spell. I know this to be a true fact because of the didn't-go-anything-like-I'd-planned summer when I determined to whip my kids into their own states of wonder. I was sure that if I came up with cool enough "A-ha!" activities, wonder would "take," and my kids would be that much closer to remembering their bliss. I even, prematurely, started a blog to detail the wonder I intended to magically embrace us all. My hubris and I quickly discovered, however, that wonder is an endogenous thing. It cannot be summoned, or crammed, or even nudged from an outside force. It must be invited in through internal, self-delighting enthusiasm. So, no matter how utterly fascinating the lecture on insect eating (and believe me, it was interesting: before that night, I'd never actively sought out bugs in baked goods!), nor how deliciously gooey the Solar S'mores, it wasn't until my kids found their own A-ha! that wonder commenced within them.[155]

So, the point is to invite wonder in for yourself. I cannot tell you your exact path, but I do know this: the invitation itself simultaneously removes roadblocks to wonder while beckoning it in. As if merely acknowledging the existence of "yes" or even "maybe" over "no!" conjures up that previously overlooked ticket on the fifty-yard line.

⌐◦

You will not question what you have already defined.

—*A Course in Miracles,*
W-pI.28.4:1

⌐◦

Here are just a few suggestions for inviting in your own wonder:

1. **Embrace mystery!** Instead of being irritated by or judgmental about things that are new and different, or that

---

155 Just another of the many instances in which my children offer so much more to me on a particular topic than I could possibly offer them!

you may not understand/did not expect, try to think about them in a new, unjudgy, full-of-wonder way. Every time we start to judge something, we cut off possibilities of Love. Instead of thinking we know it all, and judging *this* experience based on *that* experience, how about just taking it in with wonder! This can happen on all sorts of levels, from reconsidering your opinion on tattoos, to learning about religions you thought were "wrong," to trying "crazy" foreign foods (just because *you* didn't grow up eating snails or kimchee...).

2. **Study a new language.** Take a painting, hip-hop, or welding class. Learn a new card game.

3. **Sing a new song.** Literally. Find new songs and sing them! Go out of your normal song circle and listen to new ideas brought to the world through music. It's always inspiring to hear songs with messages, like "Same Love" and "Ten Thousand Hours" by Macklemore, "I Feel Good" by James Brown, "Live like You Were Dying" by Tim McGraw, "Try" by Colbie Caillat, Judy Collins's version of "Amazing Grace," "This" by Darius Rucker, and "Vamos a Celebrar" by Alex Zurdo. Those are just a few songs that have taken me to inspired places I would never have found on my own. Of course, words aren't even necessary because melody alone can deliver completely new and delightful feelings. I remember, eons ago, hearing Arvo Part's "Spiegel im Spiegel" for the first time. I was driving down the street and found myself crying: it broke me open (in a good way).

— Even better than the radio or a playlist, listen to live music. When I first witnessed Bruce Springsteen in concert, it was *powerful* and actually life changing. The songs were singing him, I swear! More recently, I thought my husband was going to lift off his seat upon hearing the stunningly talented In Mo Yang entice his violin to the sweetest high notes Saint-Saëns could ever have imagined for his Violin Concerto No. 3.

4. **Be daring.** Dauntlessly express your opinion in a Parent Teacher Association meeting. Quit a job you hate. Head to a nude beach.[156] Cook something you've never been brave enough to make before. I attempted a Pierre Hermés chocolate bombe recently and, despite spending lots of moola on chocolate and about eleven hours of labor, it was a bomb! Unsalvageable. Inedible. *However,* I gained a new appreciation for French pastry chefs; I learned something valuable (pay close attention to the thermometer); and I had fun with my oldest son who not only has impressive tastebuds, but is also a very good sport: "Don't feel bad, Mom, it was team building!" *"Failure" is just what happens when we bind ourselves to an expected outcome that doesn't look like the actual outcome.*

5. **Don't be afraid to be different.** Decide for an entire day to not care one bean about the opinions, certitudes, righteousness, or raised eyebrows of anyone else on the entire planet. There's an inspiring octogenarian publisher in New York who wears purple *all the time* (even, as she discreetly highlighted while I was in her office once, purple underwear). Don't wait until you've been here eight decades or more to live in the delight of being yourself!

6. **Move in a new way.** Try a dance class, or get your daughter's lacrosse stick out and toss the ball with her. Stand on

---

156 Or wear your perfectly-fine-at-home tankini on a beach in Italy. It's equally as daring, I embarrassingly discovered, though not in quite the same way...

your head. Feel your body move through space in a manner you've never known was possible.

— Or don't even move, but stand still in a new way. Researchers have shown that standing with good posture actually changes our body chemistry. By standing erect, chin high—versus folding ourselves up in a mousy wad—we actually decrease our cortisol levels and increase our testosterone (a "can-do" hormone).

7. **Volunteer.** I know, I've already brought up volunteering, but it is definitely an activity that plops pretty much anyone directly in wonder's lap. Every time my teenager comes home from a volunteer experience where he interacts with others, I can see the results in his face: he has felt the connection, and it is undeniably heart opening and wonder inducing.

WORDS MADE FLESH

Here's a final idea to make sure you really "get" all these Love, wonder, and joy concepts. It's a sure way to help you claim the truth about you: please write your own "book" about Love. You don't have to publish or share it in any way (though that could be fun!). Merely write to help you remember. When I say "remember," I don't mean that you should remember what *I've* written. The point is to remember what you already know, deep inside. Over the decades, I've read an embarrassing number of books about Love and miracles—each of which I dutifully highlighted in neon yellow, with Lilliputian notes squished and clinging to the margins. Yet writing about Love has helped me live in the ideas in ways that marking up other people's books never could (although I am sure that reading those books paved the way for my own remembering, and I am most grateful for that). Incredibly, while I tapped my own version of miraculosity out in the form of *Already Here*, I've learned more than ever about Love. Writing— while practicing what I've been writing about—has been a wonderfully annealing process.

What is truer than the truth?
The story.

—JEWISH PROVERB

I don't know why this is the slightest bit surprising, though. Writing things is a proven technique for learners of all sorts. I studied languages in high school, college, and after, and to really secure the words in my memory bank, to "own" them, I found it best to involve my tactile senses and write them down. In college, I would find an empty classroom with pieces of chalk still big enough to grip and fill blackboards with column after column of new vocabulary. I'd also scribble words and phrases on paper that I'd fold in half, English on one side, and French, Spanish, or Chinese on the other. The actual process of writing the words is what helped them become part of me.

Same with this Love stuff, it turns out. Write about it, and feel it in your body, and you will continue to be amazed at how much truth you can recall. Now that you have "repented" on so many levels, you no longer need to remain an unwitting Love refugee. You can find your way back to your homeland through your intention, plugging in, or just inviting your-self there…so start composing!

⟨⟩

But don't be satisfied with stories,
how things have gone with others.
Unfold your own myth,
without complicated explanation,
so everyone will understand the passage.
We have opened you.

—*RUMI*[157]

⟨⟩

You've probably already been writing a few things, if you've been enjoying the exercises. Gratitude journaling and thank-you-note writing definitely count! You don't need to make a big deal about it; just take up whatever method inspires you. Write heartfelt notes, incomplete sentences, vague and graspy wisps of ideas, bold decrees, or long and winding contemplations. It doesn't matter as long as you are doing it with Love as your intention. The physical and mental focus will help congeal your intentions into something you can see: words will be made "flesh."

The next question, naturally, is: What tale do you want to tell? What excitement do you want to add to your life? What plugged-in beauty do you want to solidify in the world? What story of glory do you intend to document? Why don't you write a little right now? Unfold your own myth, as Rumi would advise us.

---

157 This is from *The Essential Rumi*, Translated by Coleman Barks with John Moyne, p. 41.

EXERCISE 25: Your Own Happy Beginning

GO FOR IT!

This exercise isn't about a "chapter" in your life, as we previously practiced. This is about taking charge of the Big Picture you create for yourself. Writing down your Love story will help you ensure that you "own it." I now (even prior to publication) can define my life as "pre–*Already Here*" and "post–*Already Here*."[158] I am so much more fluent in Love than I have ever been before, thanks to the process of manifesting my thoughts on paper (or electronically, as the case may be).

Sir Ken Robinson, in his thought-provoking book *Creative Schools*, reminds us that "we all love a story, even if it's not true." He's so right! We often echo a story that was handed down to us for no other reason than everyone else is telling the same story— or at the very least, already believes it—so we absentmindedly assume it to be true, adhering to the ramifications of that belief. Now is the chance to write your own true story and *live* it!

1. Grab a little empty book (spiral, bound, clipped together with rusty paper clips—it doesn't matter), or open a new document on your computer, and write about the great things that are happening in your life. They can be current, or they can be upcoming. Be aware of your filter as you write, and document only the things that bring you joy...joy you can *feel*. Write exclusively about the things that make your heart smile. You could, of course, scribble out chapters about how worried you are about your job

---

158 And, yes, the irony, as usual, does not escape me, given the title...but really, the universe is hilarious!

given the economy and all, or how miserable it was to get stuck rooming with your stinky cousin, Edna, at the family reunion, but would that be any fun? Would it be helpful? And moreover, is it where you want your attention?

2. Repeat this process, including the emotional component, in whatever chunks or wafts of time make you happiest (feeling happy while intending something is like harnessing a jet pack to your plan). Try to make it a regular practice, if you can.

3. Enjoy your new life!

So, what story are you writing for yourself? If it's anything other than joy, then, excuse my bluntness here, you aren't making the most of your full authority. We are all created from the same Love that gives the hummingbird its airborne acrobatic skills, the same Love that steeps the gardenia in heavenly perfume, the same Love that imbues the oak tree with such outrageous beauty and tenacity. That kind of amazing Love is ours too, especially when we stop ignoring it! Make our story about Love, and "our story" will be Love-filled! We can recreate our reality, put a new frame around our world, and see through new eyes.

When we start writing and telling a new story about our lives, it won't go unnoticed. As I was finishing the details of this book, I got frustrated one morning with my youngest son, and I called him in for a "sales meeting." He does not like the slightest bit of controversy, so he asked me to stop yelling at him. Hearing this request, my oldest son matter-of-factly inserted, "Mom's not yelling. Didn't you notice that she never yells anymore? When we fight or do something we shouldn't, she just makes us send each other Love!"[159] Well, hallelujah to that!

---

159 Someone asked me how long I've been working on this book, and my first thought was "I haven't been working on the book...the book has been working on me!" This is an example of what I mean.

Some Explanatory Considerations

Before we finish up here, I should add a few annotative comments to make for smoother sailing.

First of all, becoming more awesome and Love-filled doesn't turn anyone into a bliss ninny, as my smart and how-does-she-always-come-up-with-such-funny-stuff friend Jessica would say. You will not suddenly glide ethereally down the hall to the bathroom at work. People will not bow down to you or give you cuts at Starbucks. You will still be living life as you, just a much, much happier version of you (and things *will* flow more smoothly, I promise!). What living in wonder/connecting with our truth/truly being does is give us awareness of peace where we are, every moment, happy, unworried, joy-filled, and unflappable. When we live in our truth, we are able, as the stunning Mary Oliver says, to see "through the heavenly visibles to the heavenly invisibles," and from there, stuff we used to find so bothersome/important/underwear-wadding will not even matter. We just don't "need" to yell!

Second, as they say in Texas, "It ain't braggin' if it's true." So, remember this: **you are the light of the world: act like it.** It's a true fact, and Things Improving depends on each of us realizing it and behaving accordingly. Being the light of the world is not about getting on any high horse or holding others in a "less-than" space because we are so much more darn holy. It's just the opposite, in fact. Being the light of the world means remembering our God-given worth in the utmost humility and helping others remember too, just by our being here and living in the place of Love. When we remember this, we can light the way for ourselves and others (because, don't forget: we are all connected!).

Finally, I must include a very important concept as we go forward: *slack*. Yes, *slack*, as in give yourself some. We may remember more than we did before, but we are still in bodies, and that necessitates some compassionate unclenching, some self-benevolence, and some slack.

Too often, unwittingly sustaining my long-entrenched tradition of duality and judginess, I still shackle myself in a cumbersome spiritual catch-22. I know what my natural state is—joy—and somehow I find myself in double nonjoy jeopardy when I "fail" to stay on that high road. At those points, I tend to reflexively grab the scratchiest mental hair shirt I can find and throw it on, cinching it tightly. Thankfully I "hair-shirt" myself less these days, now knowing how to return to my truth, aware that it never goes on vacation or offline.

For me, quick back-to-truth slack techniques include laughing, napping, walking my dogs, or cleaning a messy drawer. I try to do anything but beat myself up for not behaving in my highest truth way. (I'm sorry to say that this took me quite a while to understand, and even now, I don't execute perfectly every day. I hope you can avoid my own slow-to-learn tendencies by knowing the options!) I don't even meditate at the times I'm most self-critical. I've found I'm too far into the duality of perceiving myself as not being good enough spiritually to try and unwind that mess. No, a nap is a better reset button in that case.

⌐───⌐

You can indeed afford to laugh
at fear thoughts,
remembering that God goes with you
wherever you go.

—*A Course in Miracles*,
Lesson 41

⌐───⌐

That's all for now. I hope by the time you get to this last page, you are more aware of your innate awesome self than you have ever been. I hope you have digested the absurd ideas bound up here and now remember that there is nothing outside of you that can keep you from your joy.

Thaumaturge:
A person practiced in the art of miracle making,
wonder working.

I hope you recognize yourself as the wonder worker—the thaumaturge—you are. You are responsible for the joys your life manifests, not through some incantation to some power beyond you, but from the power you have always had within. Your truth. Really, truly, we are all already here.[160]

Thank you!

---

160 You can download all the exercises and other helpful tools by heading to KellyCorbet.com.